BEGINNER'S GUIDE TO
Shoe Embroidery

BEGINNER'S GUIDE TO
Shoe Embroidery

Everything from **stitches** to **shoe selection** to designing your own **pet** and **bridal** shoes

HANNAH MITCHELL

STACKPOLE BOOKS

Essex, Connecticut

STACKPOLE BOOKS

The Globe Pequot Publishing Group, Inc.
64 South Main Street
Essex, CT 06426
www.globepequot.com

Copyright © 2026 by Hannah Mitchell

All rights reserved. No part of this book may be reproduced in any form or by any electronic or mechanical means, including information storage and retrieval systems, without written permission from the publisher, except by a reviewer who may quote passages in a review.

The contents of this book are for personal use only. Patterns herein may be reproduced in limited quantities for such use. Any large-scale commercial reproduction is prohibited without the written consent of the publisher.

We have made every effort to ensure the accuracy and completeness of these instructions. We cannot, however, be responsible for human error, typographical mistakes, or variations in individual work.

British Library Cataloguing in Publication Information available

Library of Congress Cataloging-in-Publication Data

Names: Mitchell, Hannah, 1996– author
Title: Beginner's guide to shoe embroidery : everything from stitches to shoe selection to designing your own pet and bridal shoes / Hannah Mitchell.
Description: Essex, Connecticut : Stackpole Books, [2026] | Summary: "Packed with tips, techniques, and over a dozen beautiful step-by-step projects, you'll learn how to transform sneakers, boots, and bridal shoes into one-of-a-kind masterpieces. From playful bumblebees and floral patterns to custom pet portraits and scenic landscapes, this book invites you to explore embroidery in a fresh, functional way"—Provided by publisher.
Identifiers: LCCN 2025026128 (print) | LCCN 2025026129 (ebook) | ISBN 9780811777377 paperback | ISBN 9780811777384 epub
Subjects: LCSH: Embroidery—Patterns | Embroidery | Shoes—Decoration | BISAC: CRAFTS & HOBBIES / Needlework / Embroidery | CRAFTS & HOBBIES /
  Fashion
Classification: LCC TT771 .M573 2026 (print) | LCC TT771 (ebook) | DDC 746.44/041—dc23/eng/20250918
LC record available at https://lccn.loc.gov/2025026128
LC ebook record available at https://lccn.loc.gov/2025026129

Printed in India

CONTENTS

Introduction	vii
1 Shoes and Supplies	**1**
2 Basic Stitches and Techniques	**7**
Project: Embroidered Hearts	11
Project: Bumblebees	14
Project: Letters and Numbers	17
3 More Advanced Stitches	**20**
Project: Polka Dot Sunflower Sneakers	26
Project: Wildflower Sneakers	29
Project: Autumn Sneakers	35
Project: Sunflower Sneakers	40
4 Embroidery on Chelsea Boots	**47**
Project: Autumn Chelsea Boots	48
Project: Chelsea Boots with Daisies	53
Project: Chelsea Boots with Wheat	57
5 Creating Embroidery Designs	**61**
6 Bridal Shoes	**64**
Project: Bridal Shoe Applique	69
7 Landscapes	**71**
Project: Mountains and Sunflowers	73
8 Pets	**81**
Project: Dave the Cat	87
Project: Lio the Dog	91
9 Care and Maintenance	**94**
10 Photographing and Sharing Your Finished Projects	**96**
Conclusion	101
Acknowledgments	102
Glossary	103
Suppliers	104

INTRODUCTION

Every stitch tells a story, and this one starts in a sleepy English village. I was seven years old when I first picked up a needle and thread, while Nanna sat in her favorite chair across from the crackling fireplace. In the years that followed, there was rarely a time when I didn't have an embroidery project in my hands. The artform became a sanctuary for me. The therapeutic nature of embroidery really sets it apart from any other craft. I have spent the past few years honing the skills my grandmother taught me, using the artform for more modern pursuits. Hand embroidery is an ancient craft but one that most definitely has a place in twenty-first-century fashion and trends.

This book will assist you in completing your very own shoe embroidery projects, giving you ideas for your own designs and detailed instructions for beginner-friendly patterns that I have already developed. Whether you are completely new to embroidery or a seasoned stitcher, you will find that this book contains all the tools you need to embroider your own shoes.

As I continue my own hand embroidery journey, I hope to assist others in learning and mastering the craft. Shoes are such a wonderful canvas for this artform because they allow you to wear your masterpieces. Wearable art is incredibly underrated, but there really is nothing like finishing an embroidery project and being able to wear it for everyone to see.

Shoe embroidery is a niche that has been growing in popularity for the past few years. I began my small business, specializing in shoe embroidery, just five years ago. Since then, I have sold over three thousand pairs of hand-embroidered shoes, but more importantly, I have assisted countless individuals with their own shoe embroidery projects. There is something so captivating about a well-embroidered pair of shoes—I'm sure you've seen a pair or two on social media already! Its surge in popularity has driven many crafters my way, in search of assistance and tips for their shoe embroidery projects.

Within the pages of this book, you'll find all the tools you need to complete your own shoe embroidery project. Each pair of hand-embroidered shoes is an expression of personal creativity, and I cannot wait for you to get started on a pair of your own!

Chapter 1

Shoes and Supplies

Selecting the Right Shoes

When it comes to shoe embroidery, there are a few shoes that I find myself working with on a daily basis. Converse All Stars have been my favorite shoes to embroider for years now. They come in a range of different colors, and the shoe fabric itself is not extremely thick, making it ideal for a shoe embroidery project. Other styles of Converse that take embroidery well include the Chuck 70s and the Chuck Taylor All Star Lift Platform Converse. Both the 70s and the Platform styles are made from slightly thicker fabric, so keep this in mind if you want to embroider onto either of these pairs. A thicker shoe fabric just means a longer embroidery process and a slightly harder job for your fingers.

I would recommend staying away from sneakers made from leather and pleather. Converse makes a few styles out of real leather, and I have experimented with a few pairs in the past. Embroidering onto leather material is not a beginner-friendly project and often requires a combination of embroidery and adhesives.

Pay attention to shoe fabric thickness. Some styles, like these platforms, are made of thicker fabric that will take a little more effort to embroider.

Low canvas shoes like Vans take embroidery very well.

The elastic panel of Chelsea boots is an ideal canvas for creative embellishment.

Embroidery typically does not work well with leather materials, often making the leather distort and crack with each pass of the needle—and the process is not kind to your hands.

I also work on Vans shoes quite often, but I avoid their high-top styles due to the leather lining on the insides of the ankle areas. Styles like the Lace Up Authentics and the Old Skools are perfect for embroidery, especially if you are looking for a shoe that doesn't go above the ankle.

I will be sharing a couple of boot embroidery tutorials in this book, but I recommend sticking with Chelsea boot styles for these tutorials. You shouldn't try embroidering onto leather boots unless they have an elastic panel at the ankle—this spot takes embroidery very well, and it's the perfect way to add a little character to your favorite pair of boots!

How to Prepare Your Shoes for Embroidery

If you're working on sneakers with any kind of laces, you'll need to completely unlace them before getting to work. It's super easy to accidentally embroider through laces if you leave them in the shoes, so it's safest to just remove them. If your sneakers have a tongue, it's best to tuck this as far into the shoe as you can, as it's also very easy to accidentally embroider onto the tongue. When working with Converse I like to tuck the tongue underneath the toe cap within the shoe.

Supply List

All the items in this list are supplies that I use on a daily basis. They are readily available for purchase at most online retailers and craft stores. It is essential that you use the correct supplies when attempting shoe embroidery.

THREAD

I use DMC embroidery thread in almost all of my shoe embroidery projects, but there is one other brand that I always recommend to people trying out the craft for the first time. LOVIMAG thread is a cheaper alternative to DMC embroidery thread and even uses the exact same color key system as DMC. Each of the projects in this book will include the color number for each thread color I use, which is applicable to both DMC and LOVIMAG embroidery thread.

I only recommend these two brands for shoe embroidery, for several reasons. Both DMC and LOVIMAG threads are high quality and don't knot as easily as cheaper threads. The shine on a skein of embroidery thread is often a good indicator of how much it will tangle and knot during the embroidery process, since cheaper threads are made with cheaper fibers and often appear duller looking.

I have been embroidering with DMC and LOVIMAG threads for over twenty years and have never experienced any color seeping or transferring when the stitching comes into contact with water, which is something you need to take into account when embroidering shoes that might be worn in wet weather.

To store your thread, it's best to transfer it to bobbins or clothespins. This will keep your thread free of tangles and easily accessible for future projects. Take the end of your skein and begin to wrap the thread around the bobbin or clothespin until the entire skein is wound around neatly. Write the color number onto the bobbin or peg to make it easy to track down the exact colors you need for each project.

For each of the projects in this book, I include a color guide for which colors of thread I recommend for each pattern. I list the thread numbers so that you can source these exact colors if you want to re-create the designs pictured throughout the book.

FINGER PROTECTORS

These are a non-negotiable when embroidering shoes due to the thickness of the fabric you'll be embroidering on. Using finger protectors will not only protect the skin on the tips of your fingers but will also give you a little

I recommend DMC and LOVIMAG embroidery threads for their quality and colorfastness.

Clothespins or bobbins should be used to organize and store your embroidery floss.

SHOES AND SUPPLIES

extra grip when pulling the needle through the fabric.

I use silicone finger protectors every single day, and I can't recommend them enough. They come in a variety of sizes, and the way they're designed makes them accessible for people with all lengths of fingernails and finger sizes.

Since the silicone material makes it easier to grip the needle, I think it allows me to work even faster when embroidering—they just mold to the fingertip in a way that makes me forget I'm wearing anything. Be aware that the silicone is not thick enough to stop the needle from traveling through the finger protector completely, meaning that you can still be injured if you aren't paying attention to your needle.

Leather finger protectors are thicker, making it much harder for the needle to pierce them, but I find these more difficult to work with because they are bulkier. But if you are worried about injuring yourself with the needle—note that both ends of the needle can be dangerous when embroidering shoes, due to the pressure you'll be applying to work the needle through the shoe—I would recommend leather finger protectors.

EMBROIDERY NEEDLES

People are often shocked to discover that any kind of sewing or embroidery needle will work for shoe embroidery. There isn't any specific kind of needle you need to use for your shoe embroidery projects, though do note that needles with smaller eyes will be best for more delicate, intricate stitches.

I use DMC embroidery needles for most of my shoe embroidery projects. I find that longer needles are often easier to use when embroidering shoes because there's more needle to grab when working your hand in and out of the shoe.

There are plenty of embroidery needles available for purchase online, and you absolutely don't have to go with the brand name ones. I have a small collection of embroidery needles, and some of the unbranded ones are my favorites. There really isn't much difference; most needles will get the job done. It's more about the technique you use when

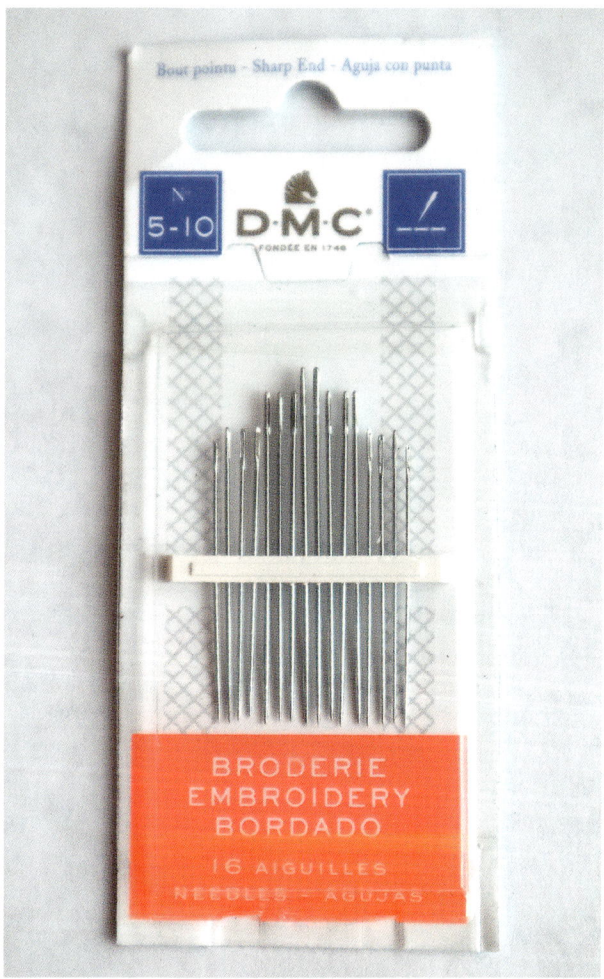

Silicone protectors should be worn at all times to protect your fingertips and give you extra grip.

I often use DMC embroidery needles, but most brands and sizes will work for shoe embroidery.

stitching rather than the brand name of the needle you're using.

STICKY FABRI-SOLVY PAPER STABILIZER

On some of the projects later in the book, I'll discuss Sticky Fabri-Solvy paper stabilizer and how to use it when designing and embroidering onto certain shoes. This sticky stabilizer can be an invaluable tool and one that I always recommend if you're wanting to stitch something specific.

There are a couple of different ways this paper can be used. The first is by printing your desired design onto the paper using an inkjet printer—and yes, it has to be this kind of printer. There are a few different steps that come into play when printing your design, all of which I'll detail a little later in the book.

The other way you could use this paper is by drawing your design out by hand on the paper and sticking it onto your shoes. If you're artistic and this is something you feel confident doing, this could be a simple way to transfer your design onto your shoes.

The Fabri-Solvy paper is dissolvable, which means once you're done embroidering over it, you can submerge the fabric in water and watch the remaining paper disappear.

TABLET/DRAWING SOFTWARE

This goes hand in hand with the Fabri-Solvy paper, since you'll need somewhere to flesh out your designs if you want to print them off and transfer them to your shoes. If you plan to sketch your designs out by hand and bypass the printing step, you can skip this section.

I use a software called ProCreate on my iPad to sketch out all of my designs before I start embroidering, even if I'm not printing out the design to stick it onto the shoe before I get to work. It's just a simple way to get all the embroidery components worked out before I go in with a needle and thread, and I think it's an essential step when coming up with something new that I haven't embroidered before.

ERASABLE EMBROIDERY PEN

There are a couple of different embroidery pens that I recommend for smaller projects and for people who don't want to use the Fabri-Solvy method.

Use Sticky Fabri-Solvy paper stabilizer to draw or print a design on and then stick to a shoe as a guide during embroidery.

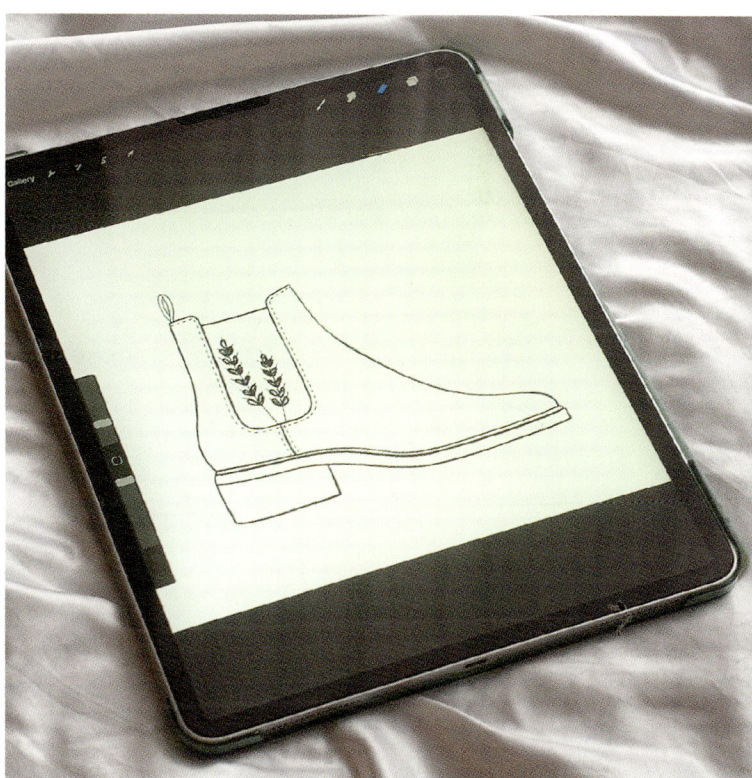

A tablet with drawing software can be an excellent tool for experimenting with embroidery designs.

If you're working on a lighter-colored pair of shoes, I recommend using the Dritz Dual Purpose Disappearing Ink & Mark-B-Gone Marking Pen. This pen has two different sides, one purple and one blue. The purple side disappears when it comes into contact with warm air, and I find it's usually gone within a couple of hours when I use it to mark onto any kind of fabric. The blue side disappears when it comes into contact with water. I always suggest using the blue side because you have much more control and your design will stay put until you spritz it with a little water. I love this pen and have recommended it to hundreds of beginners because it is so forgiving. You have the freedom to sketch out whatever you want onto your shoes, and it doesn't matter if you're not confident in your artistic skills—just a spritz of water will erase any mistakes you make.

This embroidery pen is easier to remove than the Fabri-Solvy paper and requires far less water. If you're working on a darker pair of shoes, however, you'll need a lighter-colored pen. I recommend using the Clover White Fine Marking Pen. It works in a similar way to the Dritz Dual Purpose marker, but it's white, which means it'll show up on black and navy-colored shoes.

SCISSORS

The last item on this list is a good, sharp pair of scissors. I like to use a small pair of Hisuper Embroidery Scissors because they fit inside the shoes without any issues when I'm trimming excess thread. You can use any kind of scissors you have at home, but it's important that they're sharp. Hacking away at embroidery thread with a pair of dull scissors could mess with your stitches, and it will take you far longer to complete a project if you're constantly wrestling with your scissors.

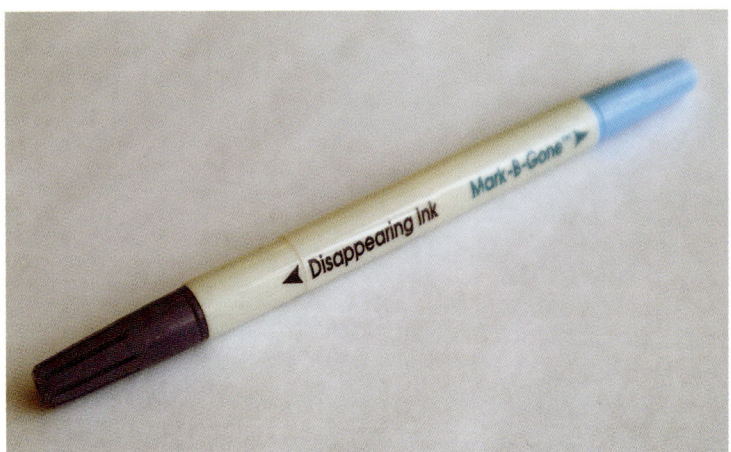

If you are comfortable drawing directly on your shoes, a water-soluble marking pen can be used.

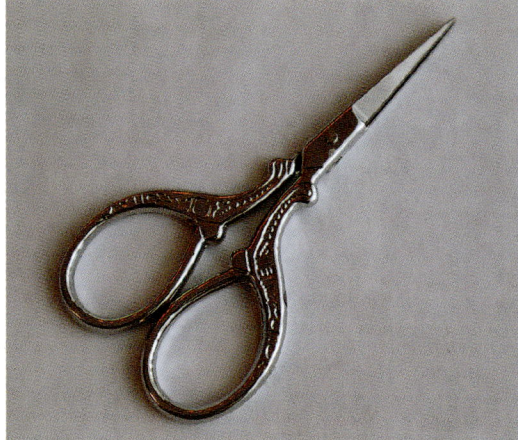

Small embroidery scissors fit easily inside shoes for trimming threads, but any sharp scissors will work.

CHAPTER

2

Basic Stitches and Techniques

Basic Stitches

Some basic stitches we'll be learning and using in the first couple of projects include:
- Straight stitch
- Backstitch
- Satin stitch

STRAIGHT STITCH

This is likely the easiest stitch we'll go through in this section, since it's usually just one singular stitch that can be used as a petal or short stem. You'll notice that there is often a bit of overlap when learning about different embroidery techniques, which is something I love about this craft. Often you might learn a certain technique and find another to be quite similar and easy to perfect! The straight stitch will give you a great foundation for perfecting other stitches like the backstitch and satin stitch!

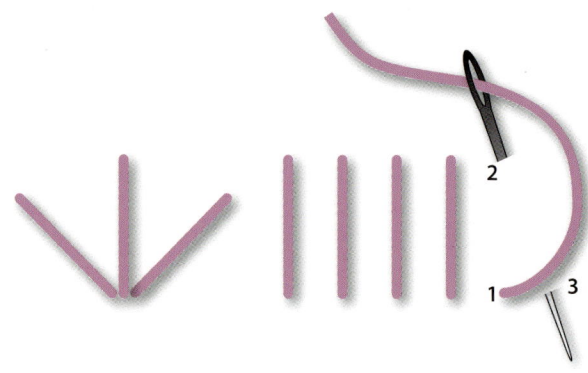

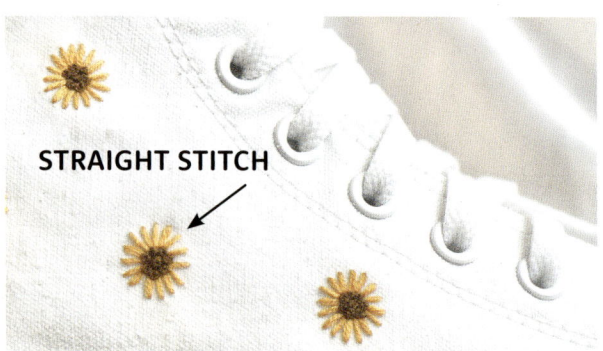

How to complete the straight stitch:
1. Bring your threaded needle up through the fabric at the apex or the base of the shape you are stitching. I don't recommend the straight stitch for longer stems or petals, but it's perfect for smaller flowers or short stems.
2. Bring the needle back down through the fabric at the opposite end of the shape and pull the thread taut. That is all that's needed for a simple straight stitch!

BACKSTITCH

The backstitch is one of the first stitches many people learn when starting their hand embroidery journey. I often use backstitch for flower stems, and it's the stitch I always use when embroidering letters and numbers.

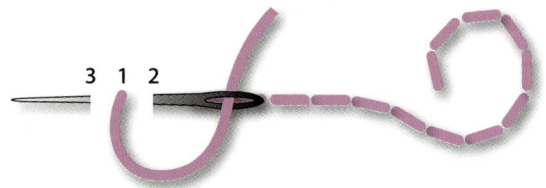

How to complete the backstitch:
1. Bring your threaded needle up through the fabric and bring it back down ¾ inch (2 cm) away before pulling the thread taut. If you are embroidering a curve in a stem or a letter, make your backstitches as small as possible for a seamless bend in your stitching.
2. Bring your needle back up through the fabric 4 cm away from your last stitch.
3. Stitch back toward your first stitch and fill the gap you left between the stitches.

BEGINNER'S GUIDE TO SHOE EMBROIDERY

SATIN STITCH

The satin stitch is one of my favorite embroidery techniques because I embroider a lot of flowers that require some nice, full petals and leaves. The satin stitch is an easy way to create a little dimension in your embroidery designs.

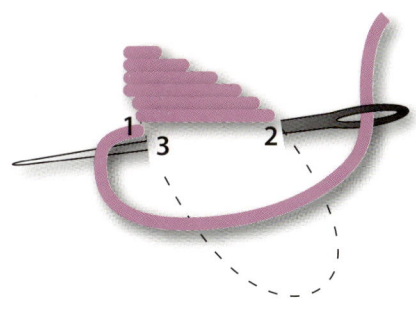

How to complete the satin stitch:
1. Bring your threaded needle up through the fabric at the base of whatever shape you're filling with the satin stitch.
2. Bring the needle back through the fabric at the apex of the shape and pull the thread taut.
3. Continue stitching from one end of the area to the other, filling the shape with your stitches until you are happy with the result. I like to layer my satin stitches to achieve more of a three-dimensional look with my petals and leaves!

USING SIMPLE STITCHES

It's easy to create concepts for basic designs when you know what stitches you'll be using for each component. With the knowledge of these basic stitches and how they work, you can put together a whole host of ideas before stitching.

If your ideas are quite simple, like a single flower on a shoe, for example, you don't need to do much planning before prepping your needle and thread. An erasable marker or a sharp pencil can be used to mark out various designs if you think this will make it easier for you to achieve your vision. In a later chapter I will teach you how to plan out more complex designs.

Before stitching on a brand-new pair of shoes, I always recommend practicing on an older pair. If you don't have an old pair of canvas sneakers lying around, then just embroider onto whatever you have handy. A kitchen towel or a pair of socks can make for great practice canvases, especially if you've never embroidered anything before. Practice most

Simple stitches can have a big impact.

definitely makes perfect, and even if you're attempting something simple, you will want to make sure it looks as polished as possible. Stitching onto thinner fabrics first can make it easier to learn certain embroidery techniques, since embroidery on shoes has the added complexity of working with thick fabric.

Techniques

HOW TO SEPARATE AND PREPARE THREAD FOR EMBROIDERY

Many of the projects in this book require you to split thread into different densities. Skeins of thread usually come in a density of six smaller threads grouped together to form one thicker strand of thread. To achieve neat, dainty-looking stitches, it's important to separate these six strands into smaller sizes—depending on what number of strands the exact stitch requires.

The first step to prepping your embroidery thread is to cut a 12-inch (30-cm) piece from the skein. This measures to about the same length as your forearm, which is the perfect amount of thread to work with when embroidering. Too much thread can cause issues with tangling, so I recommend sticking to this measurement.

To separate the strands of thread in the 12-inch (30-cm) piece, pinch the thread just below the edge you cut away from the skein. This should splay the ends slightly, making it easier for you to see the individual strands and count off the exact number you need. Use your free hand to grip the number of strands between your index finger and thumb. Once you have the number of strands secured, use your original hold on the entire strand to gently pull downward on the thread. This should pull the excess strands away from the ones you secured with your index finger and thumb, leaving you with the exact number of strands that you need.

THREADING YOUR NEEDLE AND KNOTTING YOUR THREAD

This step, just like splitting your thread, will apply to every project in this book. Threading your needle is a simple but essential part of any hand embroidery project. The more experience you gain with this craft, the easier it becomes to thread a needle, but if you are struggling, there are a couple of ways you can make your life a little easier.

Needle threaders are tiny tools that often come with packs of embroidery needles and sometimes with thread. They're used by sticking the small wire section through the eye of the needle before dropping your thread into the wire loop and pulling the wire back through the needle—pulling the thread through in the process. This simple tool can be helpful if you are using a needle with a smaller eye.

If you don't have a needle threader and are struggling to fit your thread into your needle, you may need to consider sizing up on the needle you're using. If you're using more than two strands of thread, it's not a good idea to use a needle with a tiny eye. If the thread is resisting when you're trying to get it into the needle's eye, it might be a sign that the needle is in fact too small for the number of strands you're using.

If you're working on a design or a specific step that requires you to switch colors frequently, I recommend threading separate needles with different colors. This will save you time and energy when stitching, and your project will be completed in less time.

TYING OFF AND SECURING YOUR THREAD

This is an action that will apply for every shoe embroidery project you undertake, whenever you come to the end of your thread or finish stitching a certain section: You'll need to tie off and secure your thread. I will remind you of this very important step in the key points section of every project.

Whenever you change a thread color or move onto a different section of embroidery, you'll need to secure your thread within the shoe. To do this, take your needle and hook it through some of the stitches inside the shoe, then create a knot by looping the needle through the thread before pulling taut. Repeat this process two or three times. It's essential to do this every time you need to switch thread colors or move to a different part of the shoe. This is a method I have used for years, and I have never had any threads come loose in my shoes.

PROJECT

Embroidered Hearts

An easy way to add a little embroidery to your shoes is to stitch a couple of hearts onto the spines or onto the outer and inner parts of the shoes. This small project doesn't require the use of Fabri-Solvy paper; you can use either an erasable embroidery pen or a regular pencil to mark out the hearts onto your shoes.

BASIC STITCHES AND TECHNIQUES

Sketch Guide

Figure 1 shows the general shape you should aim for when sketching hearts onto your shoes.

If you would like to embroider onto the spines of your shoes, sketch out your hearts with your erasable marker as in figure 2.

If you want more hearts on your shoes, sketch out your hearts on the insides and outsides of the shoes with your erasable marker as in figure 3.

Figure 1

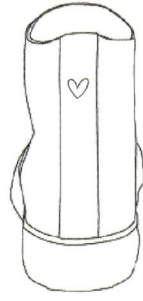

Figure 2

Figure 3

Basic Stitch Guide

We'll be going over this in more detail, but here are the basics for this design.

HEARTS
SATIN STITCH

12 BEGINNER'S GUIDE TO SHOE EMBROIDERY

Color Guide

If you're stitching a heart onto your shoes as an addition to a more complicated design, I recommend taking a color from that design and using it for your heart embroidery. If you're just stitching a heart or multiple hearts onto your shoes, I recommend warmer reds and pinks:
- #3804
- #817
- #815

Key Points

- Use an erasable marker or pencil when sketching out your hearts in your desired placements.
- You'll need three strands of thread for this project.
- We'll be using satin stitch to fill the heart shapes.
- Remember to tie off and secure your thread within the shoes whenever you move to a different area or change thread color. Loop your thread through some of the inner stitches two or three times before making at least two knots with your thread, then trim the excess thread.

Method

1. Prepare your thread: Separate three strands of your preferred thread color. I like to use reds and pinks for hearts, but you can use any color your own heart desires!

2. Stitch both sides of the heart using the satin stitch:
   a. Start at the top left side of the heart and pull the needle up through the shoe fabric.
   b. Stitch a straight line from the top of the left side of the shape to the bottom.
   c. Repeat this stitch on the right side of the heart, making sure each stitch meets at the bottom point. Do one stitch at a time on each side to keep the heart even.
   d. Create at least four satin stitches on each side of the heart, enough to cover the marker or pencil you used to sketch out the shape.
   e. Repeat this process for the remaining hearts on your shoes, remembering to tie off and secure your thread when you are finished.

TIPS

- Creating more stitches and overlapping them on each side of the heart will create a more three-dimensional effect.
- Your initial heart sketch might look a lot like the letter V—this is perfectly fine and is exactly what you want! The stitches will soften the shape, and it will end up looking like a perfect, plump heart.

PROJECT

Bumblebees

Bumblebees—another fairly simple embroidery project—can be the perfect addition to a floral design, or they can be the stars of the show.

A bee looks so cute buzzing around sunflowers (page 26).

Sketch Guide

Figure 4 shows the general shape you should aim for when sketching out your bees.

If you want to add a few bees to your shoes, sketch them out with your erasable marker as in figure 5.

If you want to add some bees as an accent among flowers, use the photos on page 14 as a guide for size and shape and add them into your design wherever you have space.

Figure 4

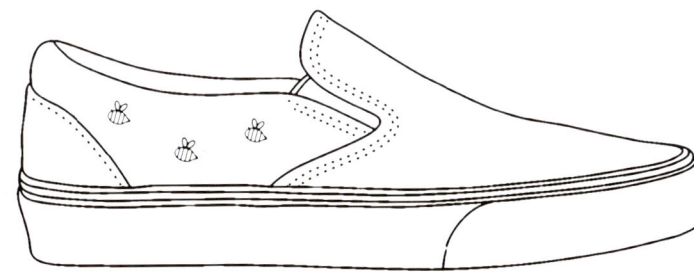

Figure 5

Basic Stitch and Thread Color Guide

We'll be going over these stitches and thread colors in more detail, but here are the basics for this design.

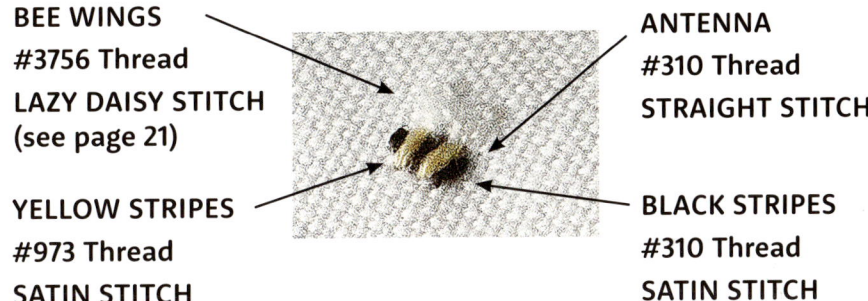

BEE WINGS
#3756 Thread
LAZY DAISY STITCH
(see page 21)

YELLOW STRIPES
#973 Thread
SATIN STITCH

ANTENNA
#310 Thread
STRAIGHT STITCH

BLACK STRIPES
#310 Thread
SATIN STITCH

Color Guide

When stitching bumblebees, I tend to stick to the traditional yellow and black color scheme with a very light blue for the wings. The thread colors I recommend are:

- #310 for the black stripes on the body and the antenna
- #973 for the yellow stripes on the body
- #3756 for the wings

Key Points

- Use an erasable marker to mark out the body and wings of the bee. It's important to use the marker instead of a pencil for this project because you may still be able to see the pencil marks around the wings if you use a pencil.
- We'll be using three strands of thread for the body of the bee, two strands for the wings, and one strand for the antenna.
- We'll be using satin stitches for the bee's stripes, a straight stitch for the antenna, and lazy daisy stitches for the wings.
- Remember to tie off and secure your thread within the shoes whenever you move to a different area or change thread color. Loop your thread through some of the inner stitches two or three times before making at least two knots with your thread, then trim the excess thread.

Method

1. Prepare your thread: Separate three strands of #310, one strand of #310, three strands of #973, and two strands of #3756.

2. Stitch the stripes of the bee with the satin stitch:
   a. Thread your needle with three strands of #310.
   b. Bring your needle up through the fabric at the top of one of the stripes you marked out on the bee's body.
   c. Bring the needle back down through the fabric at the bottom of the stripe and pull your thread taut.
   d. Repeat this process, making two satin stitches to fill the stripe before moving onto the other black stripes. Skip the yellow stripes; we'll do those next.
   e. Thread your needle with three strands of #973.
   f. Bring your needle up through the fabric at the top of one of the stripes between the black stripes you just stitched.
   g. Bring the needle back down through the fabric at the bottom of the stripe and pull your thread taut.
   h. Repeat this process, making two satin stitches to fill the stripe before moving to the other yellow stripes.

3. Stitch the antenna with the straight stitch:
   a. Thread your needle with one strand of #310.
   b. Bring your needle up through the fabric at the end of the antenna you drew earlier.
   c. Bring the needle back down through the fabric at the base of the antenna where it connects to the bee's head.
   d. Pull your thread taut and watch your antenna take shape!

4. Stitch the wings with the lazy daisy stitch (see page 21 for illustrated tutorial):
   a. Thread your needle with two strands of #3756.
   b. Bring your needle up through the fabric at the base of the first wing—it doesn't matter which one you start with.
   c. Bring your needle back down through the fabric right next to where you brought it up through the fabric, but don't pull the thread completely taut.
   d. Leave a small, loose loop of thread on top of the shoe surface.
   e. Bring your needle up through the fabric again at the apex of the wing shape.
   f. Take your needle, hook it through the loose loop of thread you left, and pull gently in the opposite direction of the petal base to form the curved shape with the thread.
   g. Anchor your lazy daisy stitch by inserting the needle back into the fabric as close as possible to where you just brought it up through the fabric.
   h. Repeat this process for the other wing.

TIPS

- The key to stitching perfect wings is to make sure you don't pull the lazy daisy stitch too tight before you anchor it—it should have a rounded shape to it.
- Taper your satin stitches for the bee's body so that the head and the stinger are easily identifiable—this might mean you have to make some really small satin stitches, but this is important so that you're not left with a square-looking bee!
- This simple pattern can be tweaked slightly to stitch butterflies and other flying insects—play around with the color scheme to embroider some fun-looking bugs!

PROJECT

Letters and Numbers

Stitching letters and numbers can be an invaluable skill and also one that you can have a little fun with if you're feeling adventurous! I often embroider future married names and wedding dates onto shoes that I create for brides, so I want to show you the process of embroidering relatively simple letters and numbers onto your own shoes.

BASIC STITCHES AND TECHNIQUES

Color Guide

I always recommend using darker colors when stitching text. If you use lighter colors, you'll be able to see the breaks in your stitches more clearly; in my experience darker colors are more forgiving and tend to end up looking much neater. I recommend using the following colors when embroidering text:

- #310
- #823
- #3371
- #500

Key Points

- Use an erasable marker to write out the exact phrase or date that you want to embroider.
- I recommend two strands of thread for embroidering letters and numbers.
- Refer to the embroidered alphabet guide for general stitching directions for all letters and numbers.

Method

This method will be a little different from other projects in the book, since I can't give you instructions for a specific date or phrase that you may want to embroider. However, the instructions below are applicable to any embroidery project involving numbers and letters. Don't forget to refer to the guides on the following pages for specific directions on all letters and numbers.

1. Write out your phrase or date: Use your erasable embroidery marker to write out the phrase or date you want to embroider onto your shoes. I like to keep my names and dates quite small when embroidering onto bridal shoes, and I'll often use cursive when working on bridal sneakers. This is all personal preference, and whatever font you use is completely up to you.

2. Prepare your thread: Use two strands of thread for neat, precise embroidered phrases and dates. I always recommend using darker-colored threads like navy and black, which makes it harder to see the individual backstitches when the embroidery is complete. Lighter colors can often make text look a little messier.

3. Stitch your text or date using backstitch:
    a. Bring your needle up through the shoe fabric and make a small stitch following the shape of the number or letter you're embroidering. Bring the needle back up through the fabric farther along the shape and stitch backward to fill the gap you left between the first and second stitch.
    b. Repeat this stitch until each of your outlined letters or numbers are stitched.
        For curved letters and numbers, make your stitches even smaller to make the curves as seamless as possible.
    c. If your phrase is in cursive, continue to use the backstitch when connecting each of your letters.

TIPS

- I always tell people that embroidering letters is a lot simpler than it looks. All you need to do is embroider your desired letter or digit in the same way you would write it—you're just using thread instead of ink! Create the character in the same way, just with tiny backstitches.
- The smaller your stitches, the better your more-curved letters and numbers will look. The letters O or S, for example, require much smaller backstitches because they have no straight lines.
- Straight lines in letters such as L and I can be stitched with a singular straight stitch if your text is small. Using a single unanchored straight stitch for text in a larger font might present some issues, such as the thread coming a little loose after wearing the shoes a handful of times.

ABCDEFGHIJKLMN
OPQRSTUVWXYZ

abcdefghijklmn
opqrstuvwxyz
0123456789

Follow your normal writing direction when backstitching letters and numbers.

BASIC STITCHES AND TECHNIQUES

CHAPTER 3

More Advanced Stitches

Some slightly more advanced stitches we'll be learning in this chapter include:
- Lazy daisy stitch
- French knot stitch
- Couch stitch
- Woven wheel stitch

Lazy Daisy Stitch

The lazy daisy stitch is one of my favorite stitches to use when embroidering flowers. It creates the perfect curved shape for petals and leaves—and even wings, as we saw in the last chapter!

How to complete the lazy daisy stitch:

1. Bring your needle up through the fabric at the base of the shape you're stitching. I recommend using this stitch for petals and leaves.
2. Bring your needle back down as close as possible to the spot you brought it up through the fabric, but don't pull your thread all the way through the fabric.
3. Leave a loop of loose thread sitting on top of the fabric.
4. Bring your needle back up through the fabric at the apex of the leaf or the petal and work your needle through the loose loop of thread.
5. Pull your thread taut, tightening the loose thread in a curved shape around the outline of your petal or leaf.
6. Anchor your lazy daisy stitch by inserting your needle back into the fabric at the apex of the petal or leaf shape.

French Knot Stitch

The French knot stitch is an extremely versatile embroidery technique that can be used to add dimension to many floral designs. I like to use French knots as pollen in the center of smaller flowers and as little accent buds on branches and stems. It's not the easiest stitch to learn and often comes with a bit of a learning curve due to how different it is from other embroidery techniques.

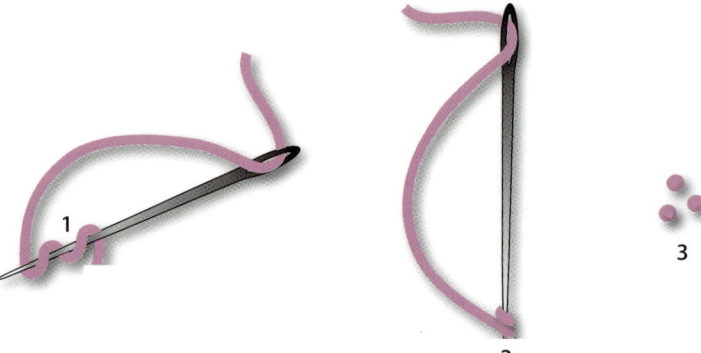

How to complete the French knot stitch:
1. Bring your needle up through the center of the area where you want to stitch a French knot.
2. Hold the needle with your non-dominant hand and wrap your thread around your needle twice (wrapping more times will result in a bulkier knot). Keep the needle pointed away from your work as you wrap the thread around the needle.
3. Position the needle as close as you can get to where it emerged originally and bring it back down into the shoe fabric.
4. Pull the thread through the fabric, keeping your thumb on top of the thread as it travels back through the fabric to control the thread and prevent tangles.
5. The knot should sit nicely on top of the shoe fabric.

BEGINNER'S GUIDE TO SHOE EMBROIDERY

Couch Stitch

The couch stitch is a technique I use in almost every embroidery design. It's often a great alternative to backstitch when embroidering a lengthy stem or a curved line. I find it to be a very helpful technique in my embroidery repertoire.

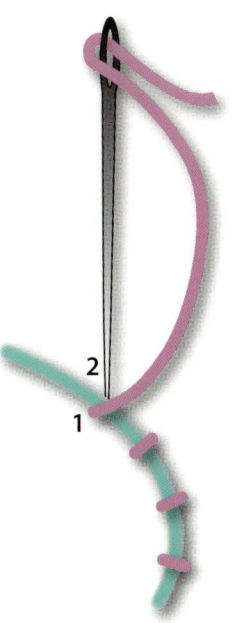

How to complete the couch stitch:

1. Bring your needle up through the fabric at the very end of the shape you're stitching.
2. Bring your needle back down through the fabric at the opposite end of the shape.
3. Travel back along the line of thread making small anchor stitches, similar to the way we anchor a lazy daisy stitch.
4. To anchor the couch stitch, bring your needle up through the fabric and bring it back down on the other side of the long stitch you made earlier.
5. Pull your thread taut and secure the lengthy stitch to the fabric.
6. Repeat this stitch as many times as necessary to secure the longer stitch to the fabric.

COUCH STITCH

MORE ADVANCED STITCHES

Woven Wheel Stitch

If you're a lover of roses, this stitch will be a game changer for you. I love to use this stitch to add a little dimension to some of my designs, because there's really nothing else like it—and it does resemble a rose when done correctly!

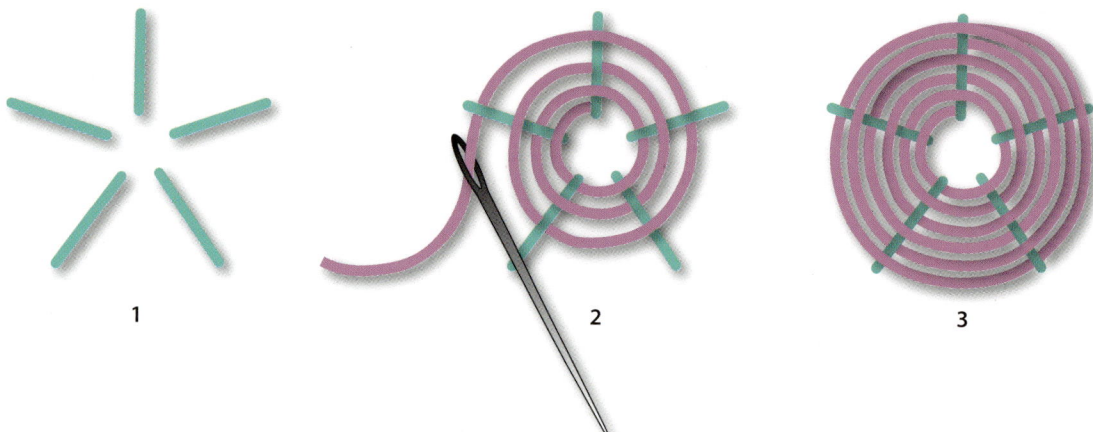

1 2 3

How to complete the woven wheel stitch:

1. Mark out a circle and fill it with five evenly spaced spokes pointing from the center of the circle to the edge.
2. Bring your needle up through the fabric in the center of the circle and stitch each of the spokes with a straight stitch. You should be left with five straight stitches, all the same length, in the shape of a circle.
3. Take your needle and bring it back up through the fabric near the center of the circle.
4. Now instead of sticking the needle back through the fabric, take it and weave it under and over the spokes you stitched.
5. It doesn't matter which spoke you start with, it only matters that you alternate your weaving by going underneath one spoke and over the next one.
6. Make sure your thread is relatively taut when doing this; treat each weave as if it is a stitch through the fabric, to make sure your rose will be neat and tidy by the end.
7. Once you get to the end of your spokes and they have been covered by the weaving of the thread, take your needle and bring it back through the fabric slightly underneath where the woven threads are covering the spokes—this will hide the stitch and make the rose look seamless.

WOVEN WHEEL STITCH

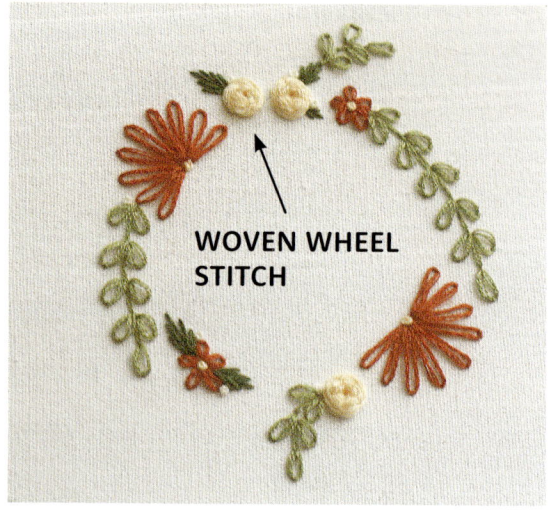

WOVEN WHEEL STITCH

Combining Stitches

When embroidering floral designs, it's often necessary to combine several stitches to achieve a final product that looks both realistic and aesthetically pleasing. The good news is that the stitches we've already covered in chapters 2 and 3 are all the embroidery stitches I use on a daily basis when embroidering shoes!

A popular stitch combination when embroidering florals, for example, would be:

Backstitch—for the stem.
Satin stitch—for the leaves.
Lazy daisy stitch—for the petals.
French knot stitch—for the pollen.

This is quite a basic configuration of stitches, but it's one that I use so often, and it's amazing how well it resembles certain flowers when different thread colors are used.

Before embroidering a more detailed design onto a pair of brand-new shoes, I always recommend embroidering it onto an older pair if you have one lying around. Embroidering onto shoes is much more challenging than embroidering onto thinner fabrics like towels and socks, so getting some practice on an older pair of shoes is always a good idea when possible.

If you don't have an older pair to practice with, I recommend starting small and building your design from there. Perhaps plan for a flower or two and leave yourself room to expand the design. Shoe embroidery is time consuming, and I always recommend taking breaks often so that your hands don't get too tired. It's easy to injure yourself if you try to push your limits, whether pulling a muscle in your hand or injuring yourself with the embroidery needle. It's far better to take your time with a shoe embroidery project and maintain a positive association with the craft.

PROJECT

Polka Dot Sunflower Sneakers

This embroidery design is simple but effective! We'll be repeating the same stitch across the shoe, which will result in a polka dot arrangement of sunflowers. If you prefer daisies, or any other colored flowers, you can always switch the thread colors to create different-colored florals on your sneakers.

Sketch Guide

Figure 6 shows the general shape you should aim for when sketching out your sunflowers.

If you'd like to embroider sunflowers on the insides and outsides of your shoes, sketch them out with your erasable marker as in figure 7. This is also a good size guide for how large they should be if you want to replicate this exact design.

Inside

Outside

Figure 6

Figure 7

Basic Stitch and Thread Color Guide

We'll be going over these stitches and thread colors in more detail, but here are the basics for this design.

SUNFLOWER SEEDS
#801 Thread
FRENCH KNOT STITCH

SUNFLOWER PETALS
#973 Thread
STRAIGHT STITCH

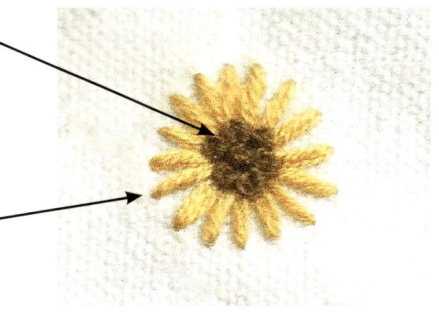

Color Guide

When I'm stitching sunflowers, I like to stick to realistic colors so that it's obvious what flowers they're supposed to be. I recommend using the following thread colors:
- #973 for the sunflower petals
- #801 for the sunflower seeds

Key Points

- We'll be using six strands of thread for the sunflower petals—no need to split your skein! We'll be using three strands of thread for the sunflower seeds in the center of each flower.
- We'll be using the straight stitch for the petals and the French knot stitch for the seeds in the center.

- Remember to tie off and secure your thread within the shoes whenever you move to a different area or change thread color. Loop your thread through some of the inner stitches two or three times before making at least two knots with your thread, then trim the excess thread.

Method

1. Prepare your thread: six strands of #973, three strands of #801.

2. Stitch the sunflower petals with the straight stitch:
    a. Thread your needle with six strands of #973.
    b. Select one of the sunflower sketches on your shoe and bring your needle up through the shoe fabric at the edge of one of the petals. I recommend starting on one side of the shoe rather than in the center, as this will save you some thread.
    c. Bring your needle back down through the shoe fabric at the opposite end of the petal, creating a straight line along the petal you drew earlier.
    d. Repeat this process for all the petals on all the sunflowers across the shoes.
    e. Remember to leave the space in the center of the sunflower free of any petals, since this is where we stitch the sunflower seeds.

3. Stitch the center of the sunflowers with the French knot stitch:
    a. Thread your needle with three strands of #801.
    b. Select one of the sunflowers and bring your needle up through the center of the sunflower.
    c. Hold the needle with your non-dominant hand and wrap your thread around your needle twice. Keep the needle pointed away from your work as you wrap the thread around it.
    d. Position the needle as close as you can get to where it emerged originally, and bring it back down into the shoe fabric.
    e. Pull the thread through the fabric, keeping your thumb on top of the thread as it travels back through the fabric, to control the knot.
    f. The knot should sit nicely on top of the shoe fabric, in the middle of the sunflower.
    g. Repeat this stitch until the center of each sunflower is filled. I usually make six to eight French knots in the center of my sunflowers.

TIPS

- For larger or smaller French knots, adjust the number of times you wrap your thread around your needle before inserting the needle back into the fabric and completing the stitch.
- Try to keep your straight stitches for the sunflower petals as even in length as possible; this will make your finished flowers look much neater.
- If you want to add a little dimension to this simple design, you can use a couple of different shades of yellow for the sunflower petals.

PROJECT

Wildflower Sneakers

This is a slightly more complex design, but we'll mainly be using the basic configuration of stitches I mentioned earlier in this chapter. With the backstitch, the satin stitch, the lazy daisy stitch, and the French knot stitch, we'll be creating a design that resembles wildflowers on a pair of high-top sneakers.

MORE ADVANCED STITCHES

Here's an alternative wildflower design. It's easy to create your own designs with these simple flowers.

Sketch Guide

Follow the sketches in figure 8 to replicate this exact design on the insides and outsides of your shoes with your erasable marker. These sketches are also a great size guide for how large each design component should be. Figure 9 shows a close-up of the design.

Figure 8

Figure 9

30 BEGINNER'S GUIDE TO SHOE EMBROIDERY

Basic Stitch and Thread Color Guide

We'll be going over these stitches and thread colors in more detail, but here are the basics for this design.

BROWN POLLEN
#898 Thread
FRENCH KNOT STITCH

YELLOW FLOWER LEAVES
#744 Thread
LAZY DAISY STITCH

PINK FLOWER PETALS
#151 Thread
LAZY DAISY STITCH

LIGHT GREEN LEAVES
#3813 Thread
SATIN STITCH

PURPLE FLOWER PETALS
#155 Thread
LAZY DAISY STITCH

ACCENT BUDS
#151 Thread
FRENCH KNOT STITCH

DARKER GREEN LEAVES
#3345 Thread
SATIN STITCH

DARKER GREEN STEMS
#3345 Thread
BACKSTITCH

LIGHT GREEN STEMS
#3813 Thread
BACKSTITCH

YELLOW FLOWER LEAVES
#744 Thread
LAZY DAISY STITCH

DARKER GREEN LEAVES
#3345 Thread
SATIN STITCH

ACCENT BUDS
#744 Thread
FRENCH KNOT STITCH

LIGHT GREEN LEAVES
#3813 Thread
SATIN STITCH

MORE ADVANCED STITCHES

Color Guide

We'll be using more colors in this design than we have in previous patterns. When you think of a field of wildflowers, you might picture a mixture of different-colored flowers at differing heights—this is what I wanted to capture with this design! I recommend the following colors for this wildflower embroidery pattern:
- #3345 for the darker green stems and leaves
- #3813 for the lighter green stems and leaves
- #744 for the yellow flowers
- #151 for the pink flowers and accent buds
- #155 for the purple flowers
- #898 for the brown pollen

Key Points

- We'll be using two strands of thread for every stitch in this design, which should make it really simple when splitting your thread skeins.
- We'll be using backstitch for the stems, satin stitch for the leaves, lazy daisy stitch for the petals, and French knot stitch for the pollen on the flowers.
- Remember to tie off and secure your thread within the shoes whenever you move to a different area or change thread color. Loop your thread through some of the inner stitches two or three times before making at least two knots with your thread, then trim the excess thread.

Method for the Outer Sides of the Shoes

1. Prepare your thread: two strands of #3345, two strands of #3813, two strands of #744, two strands of #151, two strands of #155, and two strands of #898.

2. Stitch the stems with the backstitch:
   a. Thread one needle with two strands of #3345 and another with two strands of #3813. We'll be using both colors for the stems. Refer to the photos of the finished design for exact color placements.
   b. Bring your needle up through the fabric at the bottom of the first stem. I recommend starting with the left side of the shoe and working toward the right.
   c. Bring your needle back down through the fabric around ½ inch (1.25 cm) up the stem and pull your thread taut.
   d. Make your way up the stem around 1 inch (2.5 cm) away from your initial stitch and bring your thread through the fabric.
   e. Stitch back down toward your initial stitch and fill the gap you left.
   f. Repeat this stitch for all the stems. Remember to switch thread colors and refer back to the color guide.

3. Stitch the leaves on the stems with the satin stitch:
   a. Thread one needle with two strands of #3345 and another with two strands of #3813. We'll be using both colors again for the leaves on the stems. Refer to the photos of the finished design for exact color placements.
   b. Bring your needle up through the fabric at the base of the first leaf. I recommend working from the farthest left stem to the farthest right stem and working upward from the bottom of each stem.
   c. Bring your needle back down through the fabric at the apex of the leaf shape.
   d. Repeat this process, overlapping your stitches and filling the leaf until the entire shape is filled.
   e. I find that six or seven satin stitches work best to make the leaves nice and plump.

4. Stitch the flower petals with the lazy daisy stitch:
   a. Thread one needle with two strands of #744, another needle with #155, and another needle with #151. Refer to the photos of the finished design for exact color placements.
   b. Bring your needle up through the fabric at the center of the first flower. I recommend working from the farthest left flower to the farthest right flower.
   c. Insert your needle back into the fabric right next to where you brought it up through the fabric, but don't pull the thread completely taut.
   d. Leave a small, loose loop of thread on top of the shoe surface.
   e. Bring your needle up through the fabric again at the apex of the petal shape.
   f. Take your needle, hook it through the loose loop of thread you left, and pull gently in the opposite direction of the petal base to form the curved shape with the thread.
   g. Anchor your lazy daisy stitch by inserting the needle back into the fabric as close as possible to where you just brought it up through the fabric.
   h. Repeat this stitch for all the petals you marked out earlier. Remember to switch your thread colors and refer to the finished design photos for exact color placements.

5. Stitch the pollen and accent buds with the French knot stitch:
   a. Thread one needle with two strands of #151 (for the accent buds) and another with #898 (for the pollen).
   b. Bring your needle up through the shoe fabric at the center of a flower. If you're stitching an accent bud, bring your needle up through the fabric at the edge of a small branch.
   c. Hold the needle with your non-dominant hand and wrap your thread around your needle twice. Keep the needle pointed away from your work as you wrap the thread around it.
   d. Position the needle as close as you can get to where it emerged originally, and bring it back down into the shoe fabric.
   e. Pull the thread through the fabric, keeping your thumb on top of the thread as it travels back through the fabric to control the thread.
   f. The knot should sit nicely on top of the shoe fabric, in the middle of the flower or at the end of the small branch.
   g. Repeat this stitch until the center of every flower is filled and each of the accent buds is stitched.

Method for the Inner Sides of the Shoes

1. Stitch the curved stems with the backstitch:
   a. Thread your needle with two strands of #3345.
   b. Bring your needle up through the fabric at the bottom of the first stem. It doesn't matter which one you start with, just work around the design.
   c. Bring your needle back down through the fabric around ½ inch (1.25 cm) up the stem and pull your thread taut.
   d. Make your way up the stem around 1 inch (2.5 cm) away from your initial stitch and bring your thread through the fabric.
   e. Stitch back down toward your initial stitch and fill the gap you left.
   f. Repeat this stitch for both stems on the inside of each shoe until they are filled.

2. Stitch the leaves onto the stems with the satin stitch:
   a. Thread one needle with two strands of #3345 and another with two strands of #3813.

b. Bring your needle up through the fabric at the base of the first leaf. It doesn't matter where you start, just work around the stems in a clockwise or counterclockwise direction.
c. Bring your needle back down through the fabric at the apex of the leaf shape.
d. Repeat this process, overlapping your stitches and filling the leaf until the entire shape is filled.
e. I find that six or seven satin stitches work best to make the leaves nice and plump.

3. Stitch the flower petals with the lazy daisy stitch:
   a. Thread your needle with two strands of #744.
   b. Bring your needle up through the fabric at the center of the first flower. It doesn't matter which one you start with.
   c. Insert your needle back into the fabric right next to where you brought it up through the fabric, but don't pull the thread completely taut.
   d. Leave a small, loose loop of thread on top of the shoe surface.
   e. Bring your needle up through the fabric again at the apex of the petal shape.
   f. Take your needle, hook it through the loose loop of thread you left, and pull gently in the opposite direction of the petal base to form the curved shape with the thread.
   g. Anchor your lazy daisy stitch by inserting the needle back into the fabric as close as possible to where you just brought it up through the fabric.

4. Stitch the pollen and accent buds with the French knot stitch:
   a. Thread one needle with two strands of #744 and another with two strands of #898.
   b. Bring your needle up through the shoe fabric at the center of the flower. If you're stitching an accent bud, bring your needle up through the fabric at the edge of a small branch on the stem.
   c. Hold the needle with your non-dominant hand and wrap your thread around your needle twice. Keep the needle pointed away from your work as you wrap the thread around it.
   d. Position the needle as close as you can get to where it emerged originally, and bring it back down into the shoe fabric.
   e. Pull the thread through the fabric, keeping your thumb on top of the thread as it travels back through the fabric to control the thread.
   f. The knot should sit nicely on top of the shoe fabric, in the middle of the flower or at the end of the small branch.

TIPS

- The key to perfect lazy daisy stitches is not pulling the threads too tight before you anchor the stitch. The petals should be a little three-dimensional and puffy.
- Keep your thumb on the thread as you tighten your French knot stitch. It's easy for the thread to tangle when stitching French knots, so gently keeping your thumb on the thread will control the thread and stop any tangling or additional knots.
- Remember to refer back to the photos of the finished design if you aren't sure which colors go where. There are some sneaky leaves in this design that are different colors from the stem.

Autumn Sneakers

This is the first autumn-themed embroidery project in this book, but it won't be the last! The colors of autumn are so magical that I try to incorporate them into designs whenever possible. Of course, you can swap in thread colors of your choice for this design if you'd prefer. Refer to the color guide on page 37 if you want to re-create the design with the thread colors I used. This design uses all the stitches we learned earlier in the chapter and is a little more complex than the Wildflower Sneakers (page 29).

MORE ADVANCED STITCHES **35**

Sketch Guide

Follow the sketches in figure 10 to replicate this exact design on the insides and outsides of your shoes with your erasable marker. These sketches are also a great size guide for how large each design component should be. Figure 11 shows a close-up of the design.

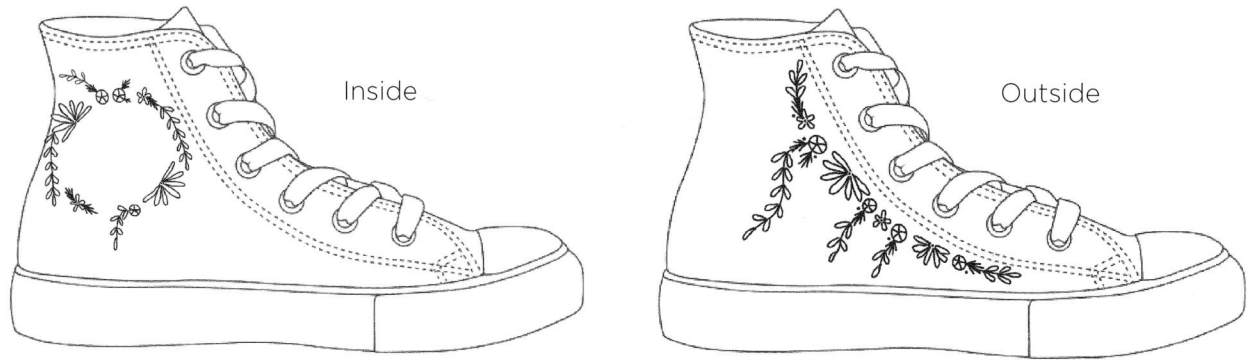

Figure 10

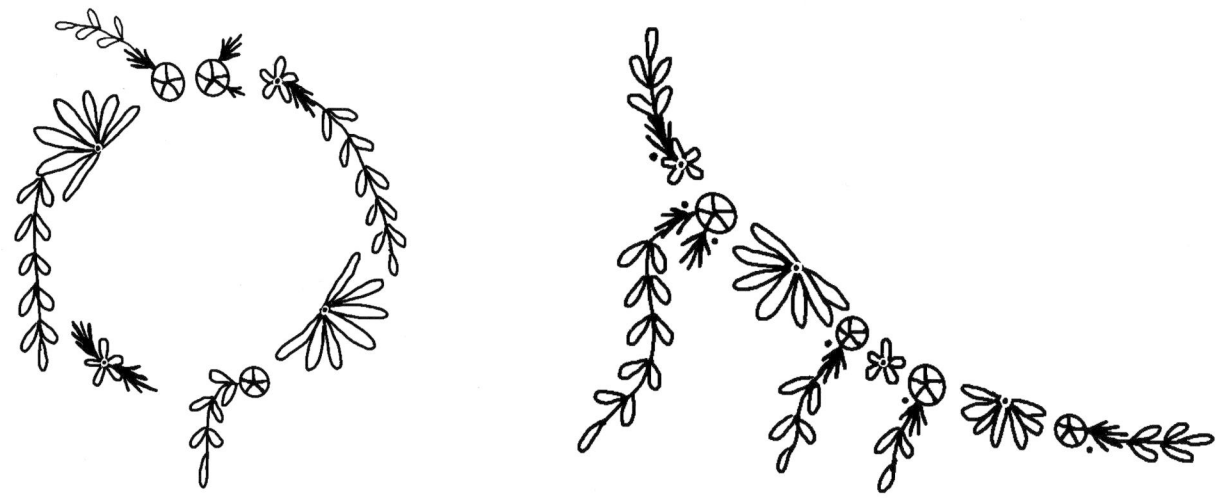

Figure 11

BEGINNER'S GUIDE TO SHOE EMBROIDERY

Basic Stitch and Thread Color Guide

We'll be going over these stitches and thread colors in more detail, but here are the basics for this design. The stitches and colors on the inner sides of these shoes are the same as the outer sides.

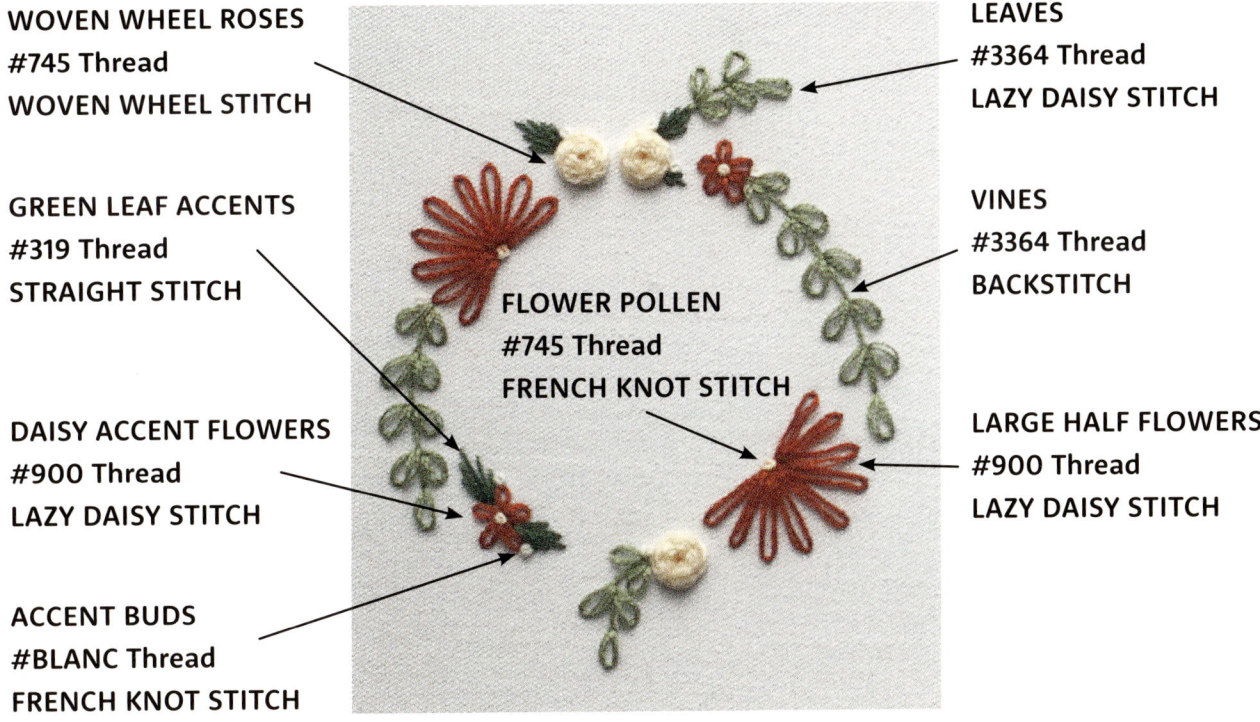

WOVEN WHEEL ROSES
#745 Thread
WOVEN WHEEL STITCH

GREEN LEAF ACCENTS
#319 Thread
STRAIGHT STITCH

DAISY ACCENT FLOWERS
#900 Thread
LAZY DAISY STITCH

ACCENT BUDS
#BLANC Thread
FRENCH KNOT STITCH

LEAVES
#3364 Thread
LAZY DAISY STITCH

VINES
#3364 Thread
BACKSTITCH

FLOWER POLLEN
#745 Thread
FRENCH KNOT STITCH

LARGE HALF FLOWERS
#900 Thread
LAZY DAISY STITCH

Color Guide

I like to play around and create different versions of this design for different seasons, but the autumn color scheme is definitely my favorite. I recommend the following thread colors if you'd like to re-create this design for yourself:

- #900 for the half flowers and accent daisies
- #745 for the roses and the pollen on the half flowers and accent daisies
- #319 for the greenery leaf accents
- #3364 for the vines and leaves
- #BLANC for the accent buds

Key Points

- We'll be using three strands of thread for the larger flowers, two strands for the daisies, three strands for the woven wheel roses, two strands for the pollen, two strands for the accent buds, two strands for the greenery accent leaves, and two strands for the vines and leaves.
- We'll be using the lazy daisy stitch for the larger flowers and the daisies, the woven wheel stitch for the roses, the French knot stitch for the pollen and accent buds, the straight stitch for the greenery accent leaves, the backstitch for the vines, and the lazy daisy stitch for the leaves.
- Remember to tie off and secure your thread within the shoes whenever you move to a different area or change thread color. Loop your thread through some of the inner stitches two or three times before making at least two knots with your thread, then trim the excess thread.

MORE ADVANCED STITCHES

Method for the Inner and Outer Sides of Each Shoe

This design is very similar on both sides of the shoes, so the same instructions apply for each side.

1. Stitch the larger half flowers with the lazy daisy stitch:
   a. Thread your needle with three strands of #900.
   b. Bring your needle up through the fabric at the center of the first large flower, at the base of the first petal you marked out. I recommend working from the top of the shoe to the toe for the outsides of the shoe and working from the top to the bottom of the shoe for the insides.
   c. Insert your needle back into the fabric right next to where you brought it up through the fabric, but don't pull the thread completely taut.
   d. Leave a loose loop of thread on top of the shoe surface.
   e. Bring your needle up through the fabric again at the apex of the petal shape.
   f. Take your needle, hook it through the loose loop of thread you left, and pull gently in the opposite direction of the petal base to form the curved shape with the thread.
   g. Anchor your lazy daisy stitch by inserting the needle back into the fabric as close as possible to where you just brought it up through the fabric.
   h. Repeat this stitch for all the larger half flowers you marked out earlier on the outsides and insides of each shoe.

2. Stitch the daisy flowers with the lazy daisy stitch:
   a. Thread your needle with two strands of #900.
   b. Bring your needle up through the fabric at the center of the first daisy flower, at the base of the petal.
   c. Insert your needle back into the fabric right next to where you brought it up through the fabric, but don't pull the thread completely taut.
   d. Leave a loose loop of thread on top of the shoe surface.
   e. Bring your needle up through the fabric again at the apex of the petal shape.
   f. Take your needle, hook it through the loose loop of thread you left, and pull gently in the opposite direction of the petal base to form the curved shape with the thread.
   g. Anchor your lazy daisy stitch by inserting the needle back into the fabric as close as possible to where you just brought it up through the fabric.
   h. Repeat this stitch for all the daisies you marked out earlier on the insides and outsides of each shoe.

3. Stitch the roses with the woven wheel stitch:
   a. Thread your needle with three strands of #754.
   b. Bring your needle up through the center of the spokes you marked out earlier.
   c. Bring the needle back down through the fabric at the edge of one spoke. Repeat this process until the spokes are stitched.
   d. Bring your needle back up through the fabric near the center of the spokes.
   e. Begin to weave your needle through the spokes, under one, over the next—continuing in that fashion until the spokes are entirely covered by the woven thread. Remember to keep your thread taut as you weave, and treat each weave under and over the spokes as if it is a stitch.
   f. Once your rose is completely woven, take your needle and insert it back into the fabric underneath the woven

BEGINNER'S GUIDE TO SHOE EMBROIDERY

stitches before tying off and securing your thread.

g. Repeat this process for the roses on the insides and outsides of both shoes.

4. Stitch the greenery accent leaves with the straight stitch:
    a. Thread your needle with two strands of #319.
    b. Bring your needle up through the fabric at the base of the first accent leaf.
    c. Insert your needle back into the shoe at the end of the middle leaf you marked out earlier.
    d. Stitch each of the leaves on the accent leaf like this, and repeat for the remaining leaves on both sides of the shoes.

5. Stitch the vines with the backstitch:
    a. Thread your needle with two strands of #3364.
    b. Bring your needle up through the fabric at the beginning of the first vine.
    c. Insert your needle back into the fabric ½ inch (1.25 cm) down the vine and pull your thread taut.
    d. Bring your needle back up through the fabric a farther ½ inch (1.25 cm) down from the stitch you just made and stitch back up toward your initial stitch.
    e. Repeat this stitch until the entire vine shape is filled. Remember to follow the sketch you made earlier.
    f. Fill in the remaining vines using the backstitch.

6. Stitch the leaves on the vines with the lazy daisy stitch:
    a. Thread your needle with two strands of #3364.
    b. Bring your needle up through the fabric at the base of your first leaf.
    c. Insert your needle back into the fabric right next to where you brought it up through the fabric, but don't pull the thread completely taut.
    d. Leave a loose loop of thread on top of the shoe surface.
    e. Bring your needle up through the fabric again at the apex of the leaf shape.
    f. Take your needle, hook it through the loose loop of thread you left, and pull gently in the opposite direction of the leaf base to form the curved shape with the thread.
    g. Anchor your lazy daisy stitch by inserting the needle back into the fabric as close as possible to where you just brought it up through the fabric.
    h. Repeat this stitch for all leaves on both sides of the shoes.

7. Stitch the pollen and the accent buds with the French knot stitch:
    a. Thread one needle with two strands of #745 and another needle with two strands of #BLANC.
    b. Using your needle threaded with #745, bring your needle up through the shoe fabric at the center of a flower. If you're stitching an accent bud, make sure to use #BLANC and bring your needle up through the fabric at the edge of a small branch on the stem.
    c. Hold the needle with your non-dominant hand and wrap your thread around your needle twice. Keep the needle pointed away from your work as you wrap the thread around it.
    d. Position the needle as close as you can get to where it emerged originally, and bring it back down into the shoe fabric.
    e. Pull the thread through the fabric, keeping your thumb on top of the thread as it travels back through the fabric to control the thread.
    f. The knot should sit nicely on top of the shoe fabric, in the middle of the flower or at the end of the small branch.
    g. Repeat this stitch until the center of every flower is filled and each of the accent buds is stitched.

PROJECT

Sunflower Sneakers

This design is a perfect example of how easier stitches can be modified to achieve a different finished look. I've included this pattern in this chapter because we'll be using the lazy daisy stitch in a slightly different way to create a little variety in the sunflower petals, which leads to a more realistic-looking flower once the pattern is complete. Sunflowers are some of my favorite flowers, and when I developed this method for stitching them, I knew I had to come up with a design where they would be the stars of the show!

40   BEGINNER'S GUIDE TO SHOE EMBROIDERY

Sketch Guide

Follow the sketch in figure 12 to replicate this exact design on the outsides of your shoes with your erasable marker. This sketch is also a great size guide for how large each design component should be. Figure 13 shows a close-up of the design.

Figure 12

Figure 13

MORE ADVANCED STITCHES

Basic Stitch and Thread Color Guide

We'll be going over these stitches and thread colors in more detail, but here are the basics for this design.

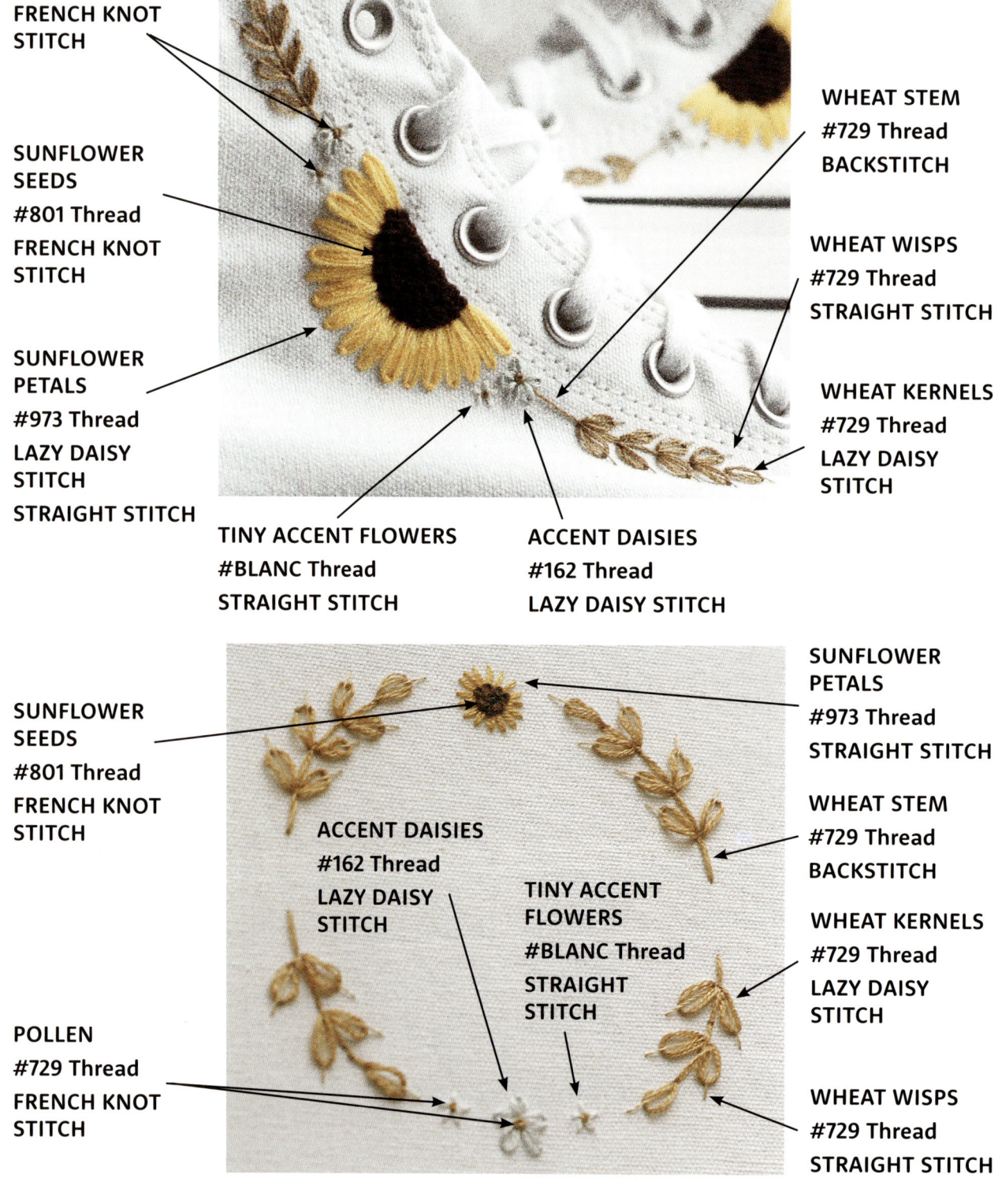

POLLEN
#729 Thread
FRENCH KNOT STITCH

SUNFLOWER SEEDS
#801 Thread
FRENCH KNOT STITCH

SUNFLOWER PETALS
#973 Thread
LAZY DAISY STITCH
STRAIGHT STITCH

TINY ACCENT FLOWERS
#BLANC Thread
STRAIGHT STITCH

ACCENT DAISIES
#162 Thread
LAZY DAISY STITCH

WHEAT STEM
#729 Thread
BACKSTITCH

WHEAT WISPS
#729 Thread
STRAIGHT STITCH

WHEAT KERNELS
#729 Thread
LAZY DAISY STITCH

SUNFLOWER SEEDS
#801 Thread
FRENCH KNOT STITCH

POLLEN
#729 Thread
FRENCH KNOT STITCH

ACCENT DAISIES
#162 Thread
LAZY DAISY STITCH

TINY ACCENT FLOWERS
#BLANC Thread
STRAIGHT STITCH

SUNFLOWER PETALS
#973 Thread
STRAIGHT STITCH

WHEAT STEM
#729 Thread
BACKSTITCH

WHEAT KERNELS
#729 Thread
LAZY DAISY STITCH

WHEAT WISPS
#729 Thread
STRAIGHT STITCH

COLOR GUIDE

For this design I tried to stick to colors that worked well with each other in a way that let the sunflower be the main focus of the shoe. As always, you can switch up these colors and go with a much brighter, busier color scheme if you prefer! If you want to re-create the design in the way that I embroidered it, I recommend the following thread colors:

- #973 for the large and small sunflower petals
- #801 for the sunflower seeds on both the larger and smaller sunflowers
- #729 for the wheat stems, kernels, wisps, and the pollen on the accent daisies and tiny accent flowers
- #162 for the accent daisy petals
- #BLANC for the tiny accent flowers

Key Points

- We'll be using four strands of embroidery thread for the petals of the larger and smaller sunflowers, three strands for the sunflower seeds, three strands for the wheat stalks and kernels, two strands for the accent flowers and their pollen, and one strand for the wheat wisps.
- We'll be using the lazy daisy stitch for the large sunflower petals and filling them with the straight stitch, French knot stitch for the sunflower seeds, backstitch for the wheat stems, lazy daisy stitch for the wheat kernels, straight stitch for the wheat wisps, straight stitch for the smaller sunflower petals, lazy daisy stitch for the accent daisies, straight stitch for the small accent flowers, and French knot stitch for the pollen.
- Remember to tie off and secure your thread inside the shoes after you complete each step. Loop your thread through some of the inner stitches two or three times before making at least two knots with your thread, then trim the excess thread.

Method for the Outer Sides of the Shoes

1. Stitch the rounded sunflower petals with the lazy daisy stitch:
    a. Thread your needle with four strands of #973 thread.
    b. Bring your needle up through the fabric at the base of the first rounded-tip petal you marked out. Remember that these petals should have the more pointed petals sitting between each one.
    c. Insert your needle back into the fabric right next to where you brought it up through the fabric, but don't pull the thread taut.
    d. Leave a small loop of loose thread on the surface before pulling the needle back up through the shoe fabric at the edge of the curved petal.
    e. Hook your needle through the loop of loose thread and pull it tight to form the rounded shape—but not too tight! The perfect lazy daisies are a slightly looser stitch than other stitches we've learned.
    f. Once you have the thread in the spot that you want it, anchor your lazy daisy stitch by pulling the needle back down into the shoe fabric right next to the last needle hole you made in the fabric.
    g. Pull your thread taut to secure the loop against the fabric. The loop should be in the shape of the curved petal you drew earlier.
    h. Repeat this process for all the curved-tipped petals. Remember to skip the pointed petals in between each curved petal.

MORE ADVANCED STITCHES

2. Stitch the pointed sunflower petals with the lazy daisy stitch:
   a. Thread your needle with four strands of #973 thread.
   b. Bring your needle up through the fabric at the base of the first pointed sunflower petal.
   c. Insert your needle at the base of the petal, around ¼ inch (0.75 cm) from the spot where you brought the needle up through the fabric—this is where this stitch differs from a regular lazy daisy stitch. The wider base will create more of a pointed tip.
   d. Leave a small loop of loose thread on the surface before pulling the needle back up through the shoe fabric at the edge of the curved petal.
   e. Hook your needle through the loop of loose thread and pull it tight to form the rounded shape—but not too tight!
   f. Once you have the thread in the spot that you want it, anchor your lazy daisy stitch by pulling the needle back down into the shoe fabric right next to the last needle hole you made in the fabric.
   g. Pull your thread taut to secure the loop against the fabric. The loop should be in the shape of the pointed petal you drew earlier.

3. Fill both the rounded and pointed petals with the straight stitch.
   a. Thread your needle with four strands of #973 thread.
   b. Bring your needle up through the fabric at the base of the first petal on one side of the sunflower.
   c. Insert your needle at the apex of the petal and pull your thread taut to fill the lazy daisy stitch.
   d. Repeat this process for all the sunflower petals. You may need more than one straight stitch to fill some of the more-pointed petals, since they have a wider base.

4. Stitch the sunflower seeds with the French knot stitch:
   a. Thread your needle with three strands of #801 thread.
   b. Bring the needle up through the fabric at the top edge of the semicircle within the petals you just stitched. I find it easier to work from the top to the bottom of this shape.
   c. Hold the needle with your non-dominant hand and loop your thread around your needle twice. Keep the needle pointed away from your work as you loop the thread around it.
   d. Position the needle as close as you can get to where it emerged originally, and bring it back down into the shoe fabric.
   e. Pull the thread through the fabric, keeping your thumb on top of the thread as it travels back through the fabric to control the knot.
   f. The knot should sit nicely on top of the shoe fabric, as if it's a little sunflower seed!
   g. Repeat this stitch until the center of the sunflower is filled with seeds.

5. Stitch the accent daisies with the lazy daisy stitch:
   a. Thread your needle with two strands of #162 thread.
   b. Bring your needle up through the fabric at the center of the first daisy flower, at the base of one petal.
   c. Insert your needle back into the fabric right next to where you brought it up through the fabric, but don't pull the thread completely taut.
   d. Leave a loose loop of thread on top of the shoe surface before pulling the needle back up through the shoe fabric at the apex of the leaf shape.
   e. Take your needle, hook it through the loose loop of thread you left, and pull gently in the opposite direction of the petal base to form the curved shape with the thread.

f. Anchor your lazy daisy stitch by inserting the needle back into the fabric as close as possible to where you just brought it up through the fabric.

g. Repeat this stitch for the two accent daisies on the outer sides of the shoes.

6. Stitch the tiny accent flowers with the straight stitch:
   a. Thread your needle with two strands of #BLANC thread.
   b. Bring the needle up through the center of the tiny accent flower you marked out earlier.
   c. Bring the needle back down through the fabric at the end of one of the five petals on the accent flower.
   d. Repeat this stitch for the remaining petals and then move on to the other tiny accent flower on the outer side of the shoe.

7. Stitch the pollen in the center of the accent daisies and tiny flowers with the French knot stitch:
   a. Thread your needle with two strands of #729 thread.
   b. Bring the needle up through the fabric at the top edge of the semicircle within the petals we just stitched. I find it easier to work from the top to the bottom of this shape.
   c. Hold the needle with your non-dominant hand and loop your thread around your needle twice. Keep the needle pointed away from your work as you loop the thread around it.
   d. Position the needle as close as you can get to where it emerged originally, and bring it back down into the shoe fabric.
   e. Pull the thread through the fabric, keeping your thumb on top of the thread as it travels back through the fabric to control the knot.
   f. Repeat this stitch for the remaining daisies and tiny accent flowers on the outsides of the shoes.

8. Stitch the stems of the wheat with the backstitch:
   a. Thread your needle with three strands of #729 thread.
   b. Start at the top of one of the stems nearest the top of the shoe and bring your needle up through the fabric.
   c. Make a ¼-inch (0.75-cm) stitch following the line of the stem; when you bring the needle back up through the fabric after that stitch, make sure to leave a ¼-inch (0.75-cm) gap in the stem.
   d. Fill the gap by stitching back up to the edge of the first stitch you made.
   e. Repeat this process and fill both stems on the outer side of the shoe.

9. Stitch the wheat kernels with the lazy daisy stitch:
   a. Thread your needle with three strands of #729 thread.
   b. Start near the bottom of the first stem and bring your needle up through the fabric at the base of the first kernel you sketched out.
   c. Insert your needle back into the fabric right next to where you brought it up through the fabric, but don't pull the thread taut.
   d. Leave a small loop of loose thread on the surface before pulling the needle back up through the shoe fabric at the edge of the wheat kernel you drew earlier.
   e. Hook your needle through the loop of loose thread and pull it tight to form the rounded shape—but not too tight!
   f. Once you have the thread in the spot that you want it, anchor your lazy daisy stitch by pulling the needle back down into the shoe fabric right next to the last needle hole you made in the fabric.
   g. Pull your thread taut to secure the loop against the fabric. The loop should be in the shape of the kernel you drew.
   h. Repeat this process for all the wheat kernels on each stem.

MORE ADVANCED STITCHES

10. Stitch the wheat wisps with the straight stitch:
    a. Thread your needle with one strand of #729 thread.
    b. Bring your needle up through the fabric at the edge of one of the wisps you drew; they should overshoot the edges of the kernels you just stitched.
    c. Bring your needle back through the fabric at the base of the kernel your wisp sticks out of.
    d. Pull your thread taut and repeat this process for the rest of the wisps.

Method for the Insides of the Shoes

There is only one embroidery stitch on the insides of the shoes that differs from the outsides of the shoes. I'll be brief with the instructions for the stitches we already went over on the outsides of the shoes, and you can look back over the instructions for the stitches of the design components we have already covered. The thread counts and colors will be the same for all of the stitches marked in **bold**.

1. Stitch the wheat stems with the **backstitch**.
2. Stitch the wheat kernels with the **lazy daisy stitch**.
3. Stitch the wheat wisps with the **straight stitch**.
4. Stitch the accent daisy with the **lazy daisy stitch**.
5. Stitch the daisy pollen with the **French knot stitch**.
6. Stitch the accent flowers with the **straight stitch**.
7. Stitch the smaller sunflower petals with the straight stitch:
    a. Thread your needle with four strands of #973 thread.
    b. Bring your needle up through the fabric at the base of one of the sunflower petals you marked out.
    c. Insert the needle back into the fabric at the edge of the petal and pull the thread taut.
    d. Repeat this process for the remaining petals, making sure to leave a space in the center of the sunflower for the seeds.
8. Stitch the sunflower seeds with the **French knot stitch**.

TIPS

- If your pointed sunflower petals aren't looking much different from your curved petals, you might need to pull your thread a little tighter to accentuate the point. This will add more tension on your thread and create the slightly more pointed shape.
- Don't be afraid to place your French knot sunflower seeds very close together. They should be bunched together quite tightly to create the sunflower seed effect.
- For the best wheat kernel stitches, don't make your lazy daisy stitches too tight; the loop should be a tiny bit loose before you anchor it. The wheat wisps will also pull the lazy daisy stitch closer to the shoe fabric, so don't worry about the wheat being too loose or three-dimensional.

Embroidery on Chelsea Boots

It's no secret that I favor certain kinds of sneakers when I embroider, but that doesn't mean you're limited to two or three styles when planning your own embroidery projects. There are a few different styles of sneakers and boots that take embroidery very well that you might not have considered before.

While I tend to prefer high-top Converse sneakers, you can also branch out into high-top Vans and even non-branded canvas sneakers. If you want to steer clear of canvas sneakers altogether, athletic shoes like some Nike running sneakers are often made of lightweight, breathable materials that take embroidery nicely. Look for athletic sneakers that are made of mesh-like materials and appear to have tiny holes in the fabric for maximum ventilation—these shoes will be easy to embroider onto.

Chelsea boots can be a fantastic footwear option for an embroidery project. While I don't recommend embroidering onto combat boots or laced boots like Doc Martens, ankle boots with an elastic cutout near the ankle section provide the perfect canvas for stitching.

In this chapter, we'll be covering a few boot embroidery projects. While I love embroidering onto sneakers, and I think embroidery can often turn a casual shoe into something much more versatile, some events and occasions call for slightly elevated footwear.

I recommend wearing socks with any finished pair of embroidered shoes or boots, and as long as you do this, you won't need to use any kind of backing on your embroidered Chelsea boots. You may be concerned about the elastic area stretching too far when you are putting the boots on, but this section doesn't stretch very much at all. I have embroidered and worn several pairs of my own hand-embroidered boots for years and have never encountered any issues with threads coming loose or getting ruined from me putting my rather sizable women's size 11 feet into my boots.

PROJECT

Autumn Chelsea Boots

This is the perfect project for those who come alive when the summer weather starts to give way to slightly cloudier days and leaves start to blanket the ground. I always feel exceptionally crafty when autumn rolls around, and I think these boots are the perfect embodiment of my favorite season.

Sketch Guide

Follow the sketch in figure 14 to replicate this exact design on the outsides of your boots with your erasable marker. This sketch is also a great size guide for how large each design component should be. Figure 15 is a close-up of the design.

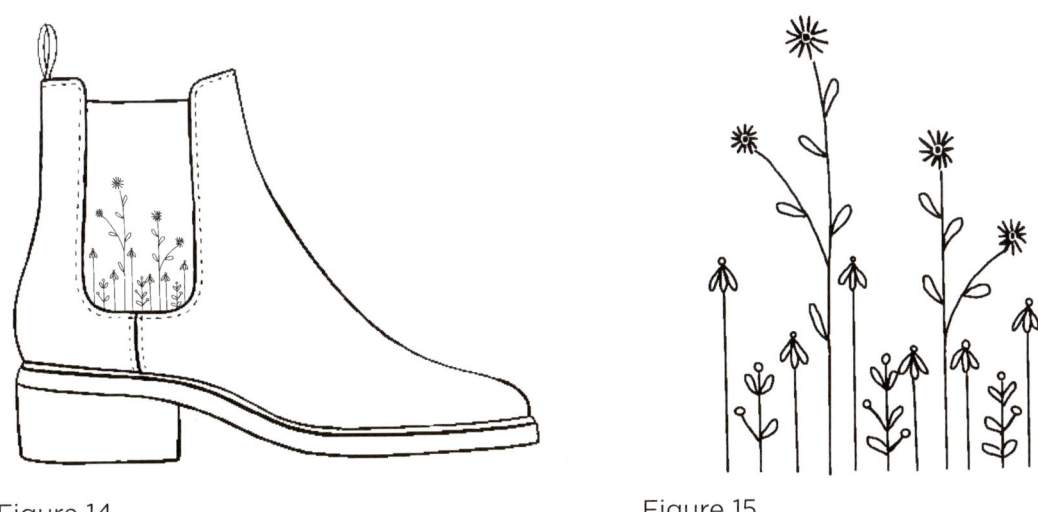

Figure 14

Figure 15

Basic Stitch and Thread Color Guide

We'll be going over these stitches and thread colors in more detail, but here are the basics for this design.

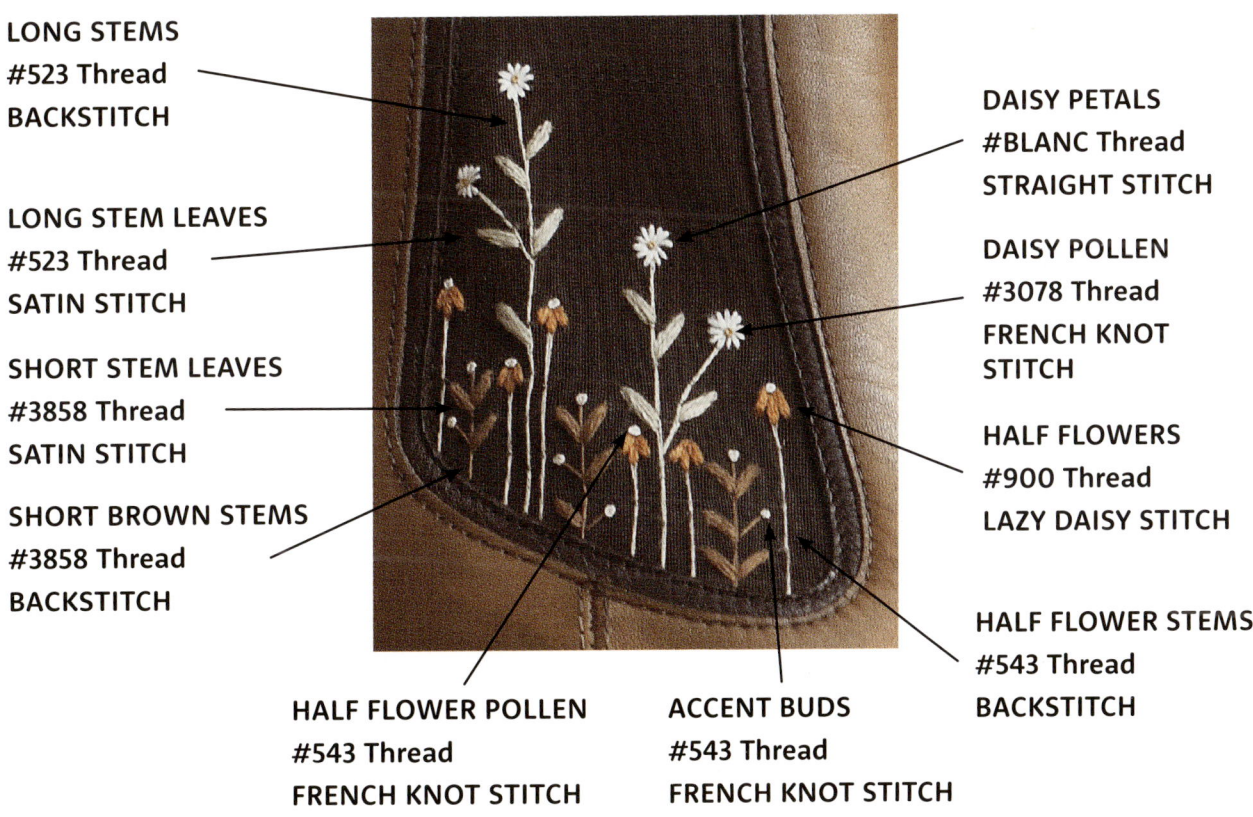

LONG STEMS
#523 Thread
BACKSTITCH

LONG STEM LEAVES
#523 Thread
SATIN STITCH

SHORT STEM LEAVES
#3858 Thread
SATIN STITCH

SHORT BROWN STEMS
#3858 Thread
BACKSTITCH

DAISY PETALS
#BLANC Thread
STRAIGHT STITCH

DAISY POLLEN
#3078 Thread
FRENCH KNOT STITCH

HALF FLOWERS
#900 Thread
LAZY DAISY STITCH

HALF FLOWER STEMS
#543 Thread
BACKSTITCH

HALF FLOWER POLLEN
#543 Thread
FRENCH KNOT STITCH

ACCENT BUDS
#543 Thread
FRENCH KNOT STITCH

COLOR GUIDE

This is another one of my favorite autumn designs, but again, you can swap out any of these colors to make the design match your summer, spring, or winter wardrobe. I recommend the following thread colors for this design:

- #BLANC for the daisy petals and the pollen on the half flowers
- #3078 for the daisy pollen
- #523 for the long stems and leaves
- #3858 for the shorter brown stems, leaves, and branches
- #543 for the half flower stems and accent buds on the brown branches
- #900 for the half flowers

Key Points

- We will be using four strands of thread for the daisy petals, two strands for the daisy pollen, two strands for the daisy stems, three strands for the leaves on the daisy stems, two strands for the shorter brown stems, three strands for the leaves on the shorter brown stems, two strands for the pollen on the daisies and half flowers, two strands for the half flowers, two strands for the accent buds on the brown branches, and two strands for the half flower stems.
- We will be using the straight stitch, satin stitch, French knot stitch, and lazy daisy stitch for this project.
- Remember to tie off and secure your thread inside the boots after you complete each step. Loop your thread through some of the inner stitches two or three times before making at least two knots with your thread, then trim the excess thread.

Method

1. Stitch the daisy stems with the backstitch:
   a. Thread your needle with two strands of #523 thread.
   b. Start at the top of one of the stems and bring your needle up through the fabric.
   c. Make a ½-inch (1.25-cm) stitch following the line of the stem; when you bring the needle back up through the fabric after that stitch, make sure to leave a ½-inch (1.25-cm) gap in the stem.
   d. Fill the gap by stitching back up to the edge of the first stitch you made.
   e. Repeat this process and fill both stems on each boot. Remember to follow the curves of the stems when necessary.

2. Stitch the leaves onto the stems with the satin stitch:
   a. Thread your needle with three strands of #523 thread.
   b. Bring your needle up through the fabric at the tip of one of the leaves you drew onto the stem.
   c. Bring the needle back down through the fabric at the base of the leaf. Repeat this process by filling the entire surface area of the leaf.
   d. Overlap your satin stitches for slightly puffier leaves.
   e. Create four or five satin stitches for each leaf.

3. Stitch the daisy petals with the straight stitch:
   a. Thread your needle with four strands of #BLANC thread.
   b. Bring the needle up through the fabric at the outer edge of one of the daisy petals.
   c. Bring it back down through the fabric at the opposite end of the petal. Repeat this stitch for the remaining eleven petals.
   d. Make sure to leave a little room in the center of each daisy—we'll add the pollen here.

4. Stitch the daisy pollen with the French knot stitch:
    a. Thread your needle with two strands of #3078 thread.
    b. Bring the needle up through the fabric at the center of the daisy.
    c. Hold the needle with your non-dominant hand and loop your thread around your needle twice. Keep the needle pointed away from your work as you loop the thread around it.
    d. Position the needle as close as you can get to where it emerged originally, and bring it back down into the shoe fabric.
    e. Pull the thread through the fabric, keeping your thumb on top of the thread as it travels back through the fabric to control the knot.
    f. The knot should sit nicely on top of the shoe fabric, in the middle of the flower.
    g. Repeat this stitch in the center of the four daisy flowers.

5. Stitch the short brown stems with the backstitch:
    a. Thread your needle with two strands of #3858 thread.
    b. Bring the needle up through the fabric at the base of the first short stem.
    c. Make a ½-inch (1.25-cm) stitch down the stem before bringing the needle back up through the fabric a ½ inch (1.25 cm) farther down from your initial stitch.
    d. Stitch backward, filling that ½-inch (1.25-cm) gap. Continue the same way until the stem is full.
    e. These stems are quite short, so make no more than three or four backstitches for each one.
    f. Don't forget to stitch the short branches you drew instead of leaves in some areas on the stems. These can be added in with a simple straight stitch.

6. Stitch the accent leaves with the satin stitch.
    a. Thread your needle with three strands of #3858 thread.
    b. Bring your needle up through the fabric at the tip of one of the leaves you drew onto the stem.
    c. Bring the needle back down through the fabric at the base of the leaf. Repeat this process by filling the entire surface area of the lead.
    d. Overlap your satin stitches for slightly puffier leaves.
    e. Create four or five satin stitches for each leaf.

7. Stitch the stems for the half flowers with the straight stitch.
    a. Thread your needle with two strands of #543 thread.
    b. Bring the needle up through the fabric at the base of the first half flower stem.
    c. Make a ½-inch (1.25-cm) stitch down the stem before bringing the needle back up through the fabric a ½ inch farther down from your initial stitch.
    d. Stitch backward, filling that ½-inch (1.25-cm) gap. Continue the same way until the stem is full.
    e. These stems vary in height, so some of them may need as many as ten backstitches.

8. Stitch the half flowers with the lazy daisy stitch.
    a. Thread your needle with two strands of #900 thread.
    b. Bring the needle up through the fabric at the top of the petal of the flower where it would meet the pollen.
    c. Form a loop with the thread by inserting the needle back into the fabric, right next to where you brought the needle upward.

d. Leave a small loop of loose thread on the surface as you pull the needle back up through the shoe fabric at the edge of the petal you drew earlier.

e. Hook your needle through the loop of loose thread and pull it tight to form the petal shape—not too tight! The perfect lazy daisies are a slightly looser stitch than others we'll be learning in this book.

f. Once you have the thread in the spot that you want it, anchor your lazy daisy stitch by pulling the needle back down into the shoe fabric right next to the last needle hole you made in the fabric.

g. Pull your thread taut to secure the loop against the fabric. The loop should be in the shape of the petal you drew.

h. Repeat this process for each of the petals on the half flowers.

9. Stitch the pollen for the half flowers and the accent buds onto the stem branches with the French knot stitch. We'll combine these two steps since we are using the exact same thread color and stitch for both of these design components.

   a. Thread your needle with two strands of #543 thread.

   b. Bring the needle up through the fabric at the top of the first half flower. For the accent buds, make sure to stitch them at the very ends of the short branches we stitched earlier.

   c. Hold the needle with your non-dominant hand and loop your thread around your needle twice. Keep the needle pointed away from your work as you loop the thread around it.

   d. Position the needle as close as you can get to where it emerged originally, and bring it back down into the shoe fabric.

   e. Pull the thread through the fabric, keeping your thumb on top of the thread as it travels back through the fabric to control the knot.

   f. The knot should sit nicely on top of the shoe fabric, at the top of the petals and ends of the short branches.

   g. Repeat this stitch for all half flowers and accent buds.

TIPS

- Don't use Fabri-Solvy paper for a boot embroidery project like this, because some leather boots don't react well to being exposed to water.
- For perfect French knots, make sure to keep your thumb on the thread as it travels through the fabric. You don't need to press down hard or apply a lot of pressure—just enough to keep the flow of the thread controlled and slow. Extra knots are quite common when stitching French knots because of the crossing of the thread in several areas.
- As long as you wear socks with these boots, backing is not necessary for the embroidery to last.

PROJECT

Chelsea Boots with Daisies

This relatively simple design is the perfect way to add a little personalization to your favorite boots. I initially stitched this design onto my own boots because they felt quite masculine, but not anymore! You could always tweak this design slightly by using some different color threads to emulate your own favorite flowers.

EMBROIDERY ON CHELSEA BOOTS

Sketch Guide

Figure 16 shows the general shape you should aim for when sketching your daisies. Follow this sketch to replicate this exact design on the outsides of your boots with your erasable marker. This sketch is also a great size guide for how large each design component should be. Figure 17 shows a close-up of an individual daisy.

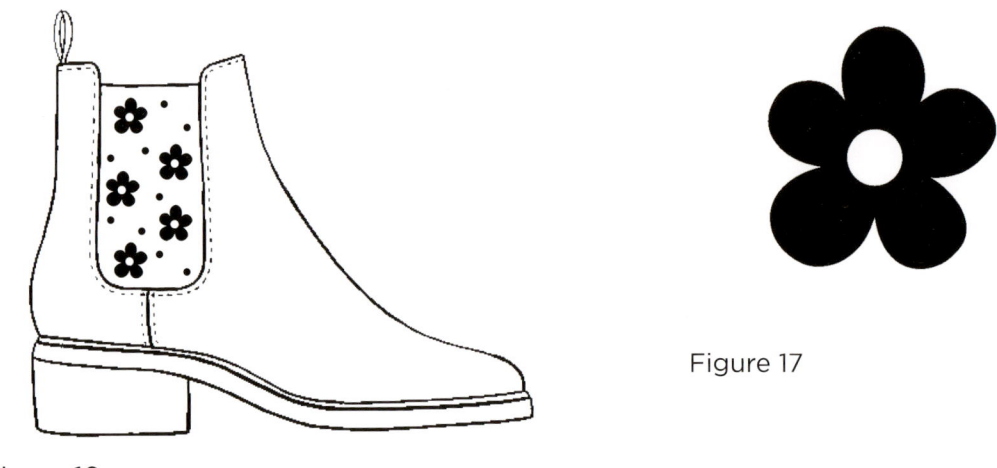

Figure 17

Figure 16

Basic Stitch and Thread Color Guide

We'll be going over these stitches and thread colors in more detail, but here are the basics for this design.

COLOR GUIDE
This one is super simple, just two colors! Which makes it even easier to swap other colors in if you would like a pop of color in this design. The thread colors I recommend for this design include:
- #5200 for daisy petals and accent dots
- #743 for the pollen in the center of the daisies

ACCENT DOTS
#5200 Thread
FRENCH KNOT STITCH

POLLEN
#743 Thread
FRENCH KNOT STITCH

DAISY PETALS
#5200 Thread
SATIN STITCH

54 BEGINNER'S GUIDE TO SHOE EMBROIDERY

Key Points

- We'll be using four strands of embroidery thread to fill in the daisies and two strands of embroidery thread for the pollen and small accents.
- We'll be using the satin stitch to fill the daisies and the French knot stitch for the pollen and accents.
- Remember to tie off and secure your thread inside the boots after you complete each step. Loop your thread through some of the inner stitches two or three times before making at least two knots with your thread, then trim the excess thread.

Method

1. Stitch the daisies with the satin stitch:
    a. Thread your needle with four strands of #5200 thread.
    b. Bring the needle up through the fabric at the edge of one of the daisies. It doesn't matter which one you start with, but try to work your way from either the top or bottom to conserve thread.
    c. Take your needle and bring it back down through the fabric at the center of the daisy, creating a straight stitch from the apex of the petal to the middle of the flower.
    d. Repeat this process for each of the petals on each daisy shape. This satin stitch is a little different from the way we used it to fill in leaves on previous projects. For this stitch you'll have to remember to angle your stitches so they all converge in the middle of the flower while also overlapping your stitches to achieve more of a three-dimensional effect.
    e. I find that at least eight satin stitches on each petal look best for plump petals.

2. Stitch the pollen with the French knot stitch:
    a. Thread your needle with two strands of #743 thread.
    b. Bring the needle up through the fabric at the center of the daisy.
    c. Hold the needle with your non-dominant hand and loop your thread around your needle twice. Keep the needle pointed away from your work as you loop the thread around it.
    d. Position the needle as close as you can get to where it emerged originally, and bring it back down into the shoe fabric.
    e. Pull the thread through the fabric, keeping your thumb on top of the thread as it travels back through the fabric to control the knot.
    f. The knot should sit nicely on top of the fabric, in the middle of the flower.
    g. Repeat this stitch in the center of the remaining daisy flowers.

3. Stitch the accent dots with the French knot stitch:
    a. Thread your needle with two strands of #5200 thread.
    b. Bring the needle up through the fabric at one of the dots you marked out earlier. It doesn't matter which one you start with, but try to stitch them in order of which is closest to the one you just finished so you don't jump from one at the very top to one at the bottom.
    c. Hold the needle with your non-dominant hand and loop your thread around your needle twice. Keep the needle pointed away from your work as you loop the thread around it.
    d. Position the needle as close as you can get to where it emerged originally, and bring it back down into the shoe fabric.
    e. Pull the thread through the fabric, keeping your thumb on top of the thread as it travels back through the fabric to control the knot.

f. The knot should sit nicely on top of the shoe fabric, as if it's a tiny petal floating in the wind.

g. Repeat this stitch for all the dots you marked out earlier.

TIPS

- For slightly larger French knots, just wrap the thread around the needle once or twice more before sticking the needle back into the fabric and securing the knot.
- Always keep a fair amount of tension on the thread when you are stitching a French knot. I find it best to rest my thumb on the thread as it travels back through the fabric so that no extra knots form.
- If you do have any issues with thread tangling while stitching French knots, it's best to cut your losses and rethread your needle. The French knot stitch is not easy, and I often find my thread tangling and forming extra knots when I'm not being super careful—this is ok! Just snip off any excess thread and start fresh from the spot you were working on.

PROJECT

Chelsea Boots with Wheat

This design is the perfect way to add a little whimsy to your boots without spending weeks on an embroidery project. When I finished this project, I couldn't believe how much the stitches looked like they belonged on the ankle section, and it took me less than two hours to finish both of the boots—a win in my book!

EMBROIDERY ON CHELSEA BOOTS

Sketch Guide

Figure 18 shows the general shape you should aim for when sketching out your wheat sprigs. Follow this sketch to replicate this exact design on the outsides of your boots with your erasable marker. This sketch is also a great size guide for how large each design component should be. Figure 19 shows a close-up of wheat sprigs.

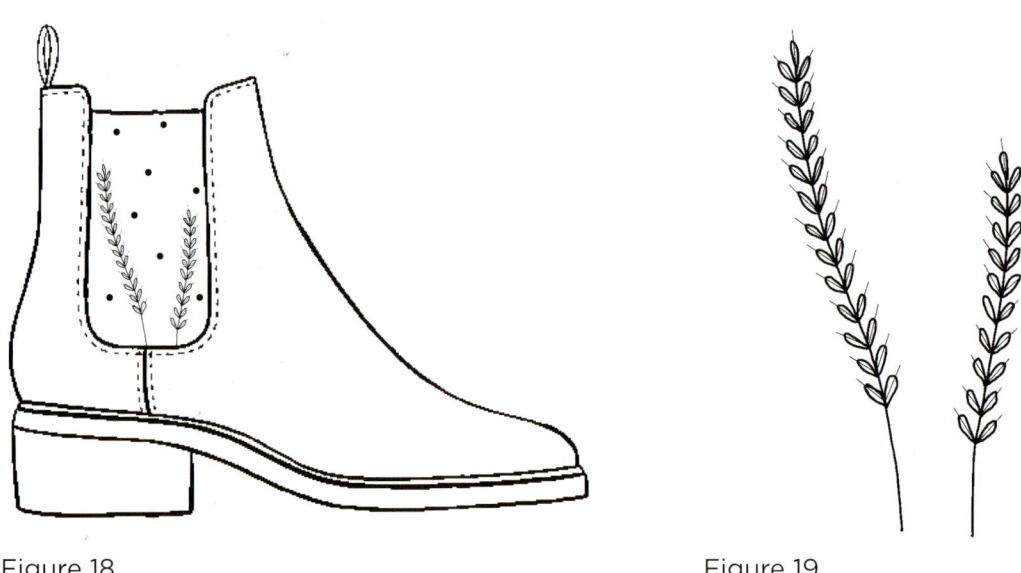

Figure 18

Figure 19

Basic Stitch and Thread Color Guide

We'll be going over these stitches and thread colors in more detail, but here are the basics for this design.

WHEAT WISPS
#3866 Thread
STRAIGHT STITCH

WHEAT KERNELS
#3859 Thread
LAZY DAISY STITCH

ACCENT DOTS
#BLANC Thread
FRENCH KNOT STITCH

WHEAT STEMS
#3866 Thread
BACKSTITCH

COLOR GUIDE

This is another fairly simple design using just three different colors of thread! I recommend the following thread colors for this pattern:
- #3866 for the stems and wheat wisps
- #3859 for the wheat kernels
- #BLANC for the accent dots

Key Points

- We'll be using two strands of embroidery thread for the wheat stems and accent dots, four strands for the kernels, and one strand for the kernel wisps.
- We'll be using the backstitch for the stems, lazy daisy stitch for the kernels, straight stitch for the wisps, and French knot stitch for the accent dots.
- Remember to tie off and secure your thread inside the boots after you complete each step. Loop your thread through some of the inner stitches two or three times before making at least two knots with your thread, then trim the excess thread.

Method

1. Stitch the wheat stems with the backstitch:
   a. Thread your needle with two strands of #3866 thread.
   b. Start at the top of one of the stems and bring your needle up through the fabric. It doesn't matter which stem you start with.
   c. Make a ½-inch (1.25-cm) stitch following the line of the stem; when you bring the needle back up through the fabric after that stitch, make sure to leave a ½-inch (1.25-cm) gap in the stem.
   d. Fill the gap by stitching back up to the edge of the first stitch you made.
   e. Repeat this process and fill both stems on each boot. Remember to follow the curves of the stems when necessary.

2. Stitch the kernels with the lazy daisy stitch:
   a. Thread your needle with four strands of #3859 thread.
   b. Start at the bottom of one of the stems and bring your needle up through the fabric at the base of the first kernel you sketched out.
   c. Insert your needle back into the fabric right next to where you brought it up through the fabric, but don't pull the thread taut.
   d. Leave a small loop of loose thread on the surface before pulling the needle back up through the shoe fabric at the edge of the wheat kernel you drew earlier.
   e. Hook your needle through the loop of loose thread and pull it tight to form the rounded shape—not too tight! The perfect lazy daisies are a slightly looser stitch than other stitches we've learned.
   f. Once you have the thread in the spot that you want it, anchor your lazy daisy stitch by pulling the needle back down into the shoe fabric right next to the last needle hole you made in the fabric.
   g. Pull your thread taut to secure the loop against the fabric. The loop should be in the shape of the kernel you drew.
   h. Repeat this process for all the wheat kernels on each stem.

3. Stitch the wisps on each of the kernels with the straight stitch:
   a. Thread your needle with one strand of #3866 thread.
   b. Bring your needle up through the fabric at the edge of one of the wisps you drew. I find starting at the base of the stems easier.
   c. Bring your needle back through the fabric at the base of the kernel your wisp sticks out of.

d. Pull your thread taut. Repeat this process for the rest of the wisps.

4. Stitch the accent dots with the French knot stitch:
   a. Thread your needle with two strands of #BLANC thread.
   b. Bring the needle up through the fabric at one of the dots you marked out earlier. It doesn't matter which one you start with, but try to stitch them in order of which is closest to the one you just finished so you don't jump from one at the very top to one at the bottom.
   c. Hold the needle with your non-dominant hand and loop your thread around your needle twice. Keep the needle pointed away from your work as you loop the thread around it.
   d. Position the needle as close as you can get to where it emerged originally, and bring it back down into the shoe fabric.
   e. Pull the thread through the fabric, keeping your thumb on top of the thread as it travels back through the fabric to control the knot.
   f. The knot should sit nicely on top of the shoe fabric, as if it's a tiny speck of wheat floating in the wind.
   g. Repeat this stitch for all the dots you marked out earlier.

TIPS

- The wisps seem like a small step, but they pull this design together so nicely! Try to keep them as uniform as possible and follow the sketch you made on the boots as closely as you can for the best results.
- Don't pull your lazy daisy stitches too tight. They should be slightly puffy, especially on this design where we use four strands of thread for the kernels.
- Remember to switch your thread colors! This seems like a simple tip, but since we are using similar colors for most of the stitches in this design, it can be easy to forget to change thread colors between steps.

Creating Embroidery Designs

You may be pursuing shoe embroidery as a craft because you have your own design ideas that you'd like to bring to life on a pair of shoes. This is something I always encourage, especially if there's a specific flower or greenery you'd like to incorporate into a floral design. If this is the case, there are a few different ways you can design your own shoe embroidery patterns. These include:
- Pencil and paper
- Digital sketching software
- Sticky Fabri-Solvy stabilizer paper

Design Methods

PENCIL AND PAPER
This may seem a little obvious, but it's the way most of my best-selling designs were brought to life! There's something special about getting your idea down on paper, even if you have to erase parts of it several times before you're happy with it. I always recommend trying to outline the shape of the shoe you want to embroider onto and then adding your design to the paper. This is a great way to make sure there's room for everything you want to add. By getting your ideas down on paper, you can visualize the end product and even plan specific stitches based on the components you want to embroider.

DIGITAL SKETCHING SOFTWARE
This is a relatively new addition to my creative process but one that I would highly recommend to anyone with a tablet or laptop. This option carries all the benefits of sketching your design out on paper, except it's on a screen and you have so many additional tools at your disposal. I like to use ProCreate on my iPad, and it's revolutionized the way I sketch out my designs. Online marketplaces such as Etsy have all kinds of digital stamps available for software like this, so if you want to add a certain flower into your design but you aren't confident in your ability to sketch it, you'll more than likely be able to find a digital stamp that you can download and use when sketching your design. This option is

also perfect for people who find it harder to get their ideas down on paper. I happen to be one of those people, and though embroidery is an artform I consider myself to be skilled in, I am no sketch artist! The freedom ProCreate has given me to sketch out whatever comes to mind with ease has been a game changer, since I like to release a few new designs each year and am constantly coming up with new ideas.

STICKY FABRI-SOLVY STABILIZER PAPER

Whether you draw your designs out on paper or use digital sketching software, Fabri-Solvy paper can be used to transfer your design onto your shoes. Sticky Fabri-Solvy paper is an adhesive, water-soluble paper that you can either print or draw directly onto. Once you've embroidered your design and the Fabri-Solvy paper has served its purpose, you just expose the design to water and the paper will dissolve, leaving you with a finished embroidery project.

Since I started using ProCreate, I've been printing directly onto Fabri-Solvy, and I can't say enough good things about it! It's such a fantastic way to transfer your exact design onto your shoes. If using digital software and printing onto Fabri-Solvy paper sounds like the route you want to take, you'll need an inkjet printer—this is the only kind of printer that works with the paper, which is something to keep in mind if you don't already own one. The paper comes in printable sheets, but it also comes in larger rolls that you can cut down to size.

If using digital software and printing your designs sound a little complex, don't fret! You can also sketch directly onto the Fabri-Solvy paper! This is a method I have used in the past and it works perfectly well. I recommend using a pencil and lightly sketching your design onto the paper; you could even trace a design you have already created. The process of sticking your design onto the shoes and stitching over it is exactly the same, as is the process of removing the soluble paper with water once you're finished embroidering. This method is more cost-effective than the digital route, especially if you don't have access to a tablet or an inkjet printer.

And of course, the erasable embroidery marker is always an option, even for more complex designs. If you're confident in your artistic abilities and feel that you can sketch your design directly onto the shoes with an erasable marker—go for it! You'll be saving yourself

Draw or print your sketch onto Fabri-Solvy paper.

The paper will stick to the shoe as a reference while you embroider and then dissolve away with a little water.

a lot of time and effort, and even if you make a mistake, you can just erase the marker with some water.

Key Points When Designing Your Own Embroidery Patterns

- The kind of shoe you're working with
- The equipment you have access to
- The amount of work you want to put into your shoe embroidery project

The kind of shoe you're working with will determine the layout of your design as well as how much embroidery you can do on the shoes. If you have a low-top pair of Converses, you'll be able to embroider far less onto the shoes than if you have a pair of high tops. I always recommend designing your pattern to work with the layout of the shoe. For example, if you're embroidering onto a pair of high-top Converses, you'll notice there's a round logo on the inner sides of the shoes—I like to work my designs around this rather than ignoring its existence or attempting to embroider through it.

You also need to note that there are certain areas on the shoes that you should avoid embroidering. Most shoes have some kind of rubber inset in the heel area to support the back of your foot. This area should be avoided at all costs—it's almost impossible to get the needle through this part of the shoe, and you're more likely to injure yourself by attempting it. I'd also recommend steering clear of any parts of the shoe that feel much thicker than others. This could be a seam area or any spot on the shoes where it looks like material has overlapped during the manufacturing process. It will be a lot harder to get your needle through these areas, so working your design around these parts of the shoe will make the entire shoe embroidery process much more enjoyable.

The equipment you have access to will play a part in the way you design and transfer your design onto your shoes. This is important if you don't have a lot of faith in your ability to take an erasable marker and sketch a pattern directly onto your shoes. Using digital sketching software like ProCreate is fantastic, but if you have no way of printing your design and no Fabri-Solvy paper, it might be best to use a pen and paper or sketch directly onto your shoes with an erasable marker. If you do have access to ProCreate, Fabri-Solvy paper, and an inkjet printer, you may be able to produce designs of higher quality. With the help of downloadable art stamps, designing detailed floral embroidery patterns has never been easier.

The amount of work you want to put into your shoe embroidery project is also a consideration. If you just want to add a small heart or a bumblebee to your shoes, your project won't take more than an hour to complete. If you have something more detailed in mind, make sure you plan out each of the design components. If you look closely at some of my designs, many of them don't cover a large portion of the shoe. This is done purposely, since I embroider shoes daily and often need to be able to produce two to three pairs within the span of one day. If you design your pattern well, you won't have to completely fill the shoe with embroidery for the design to be aesthetically pleasing. You'll see that many of my designs focus on a certain area of the shoe. I have many designs that span the length of the laces or appear to grow from the sole of the shoe. Don't fret about filling every bit of space on the shoe with stitches; focus more on the kind of flowers and specific stitches you want to use on your shoes.

Chapter 6

Bridal Shoes

Hand-embroidered shoes have become extremely popular with brides over the past few years. Most of my clientele are brides, and I increasingly find myself developing more wedding-related designs. This often means adding a few extra embellishments to each shoe, or even hand-stitching lace and other appliques onto the shoes to match veils and wedding dresses.

If you'd like to add a bridal touch to your own shoes, you could consider:
- Beaded pearls, rhinestones, and sequins
- Lace and appliques
- Alternate laces

Rhinestones and gems can be a fantastic way to add sparkle and dimension to a pair of sneakers. You can use them in addition to an embroidery design or have them be the main focus of the design by securing them with thread all over the shoes. A floral arrangement with offshoots of foliage is relatively easy to achieve with rhinestones of different sizes.

Using a metallic thread for names and dates on the back of the shoes can add a little extra sparkle.

Matching your shoes to the color scheme of your wedding can be a fun, personal project to embark upon.

Using more muted thread colors with similar hues will make your overall design look more cohesive and natural. If you have quite a busy color scheme, consider choosing three or four colors from it and working with those to embroider your bridal shoes.

Beaded Pearls, Rhinestones, and Sequins

Pearls can be incorporated into any floral hand embroidery design in the place of petals or pollen, but I also like to add them when filling small spaces between flowers or other design components. The same goes for rhinestones, though I use these a little more sparingly in my own designs because they contrast with the white bridal sneakers more than the pearls do. I recommend varying the sizes of your embellishments to add more dimension to the design. It can look a little flat when you only use one size across both shoes. Sequins are an addition I use sparingly, but I find they can look extremely elegant when combined with other beads.

There are flatback pearls and rhinestones, but I use beaded versions of these embellishments when incorporating them into my designs.

BRIDAL SHOES

This is because the flatback versions need to be glued, whereas the beaded versions can be attached to the shoes using thread. Embroidering pearls and rhinestones onto your shoes is a much safer option because glue is nowhere near as reliable as thread. If the shoes are used for wedding night revelry and saved for years after the big day as a keepsake, embroidering the embellishments will ensure everything stays in place.

Lace and Appliques

Many bridal accessories, like veils, are made from embroidered fabrics that can also be used to add smaller embellishments to shoes. I have embroidered countless shoes with appliques like these to match veils and other accessories, though I find they often look best when incorporated into a hand-embroidered design. I often add beaded embellishments

Rhinestones can really add character and bling to a relatively plain pair of shoes. Since we're not able to use a leather punch on the soles of the shoes, a strong adhesive is required to secure the design to the soles of the shoes. I prefer to use a needle and thread where possible, but an adhesive like methyl methacrylate is best when working with shoes.

Pearls match white shoes for a more understated, feminine design.

Exploring different ways to assemble pearls can be a fun way to add more dimension to your designs. Consider making a flower out of different pearl shapes!

BEGINNER'S GUIDE TO SHOE EMBROIDERY

when creating shoes like this to tie the components together and make everything look cohesive on the shoes.

One way to honor a loved one is to incorporate part of their wedding dress or veil into your own accessories on your big day. I have taken many cuts of lace and older appliques and incorporated them into hand-embroidered designs on bridal sneakers. Much like in the case of beaded embellishments, I always recommend embroidering lace or appliques onto the shoes rather than glueing.

Adding older lace to shoes may involve delicately cutting around certain parts of the design that you like in a shape that will work with the shoe you plan to embroider. It will help to measure the shoe and outline exactly what you want on the outer part of the shoe and what might work on the inside of the shoe. Keep in mind that there are two shoes. You will have to decide whether or not you want them both to look exactly the same—which might prove difficult if you are working with a limited amount of older fabric.

Appliques and other embellishments can greatly add to a bridal shoe. If you have lace or an applique that matches your dress, you can use a combination of a leather punch, embroidery thread, and strong adhesive (I recommend methyl methacrylate) to attach it to your shoes. Since leather shoes are extremely thick, you will need a leather punch in order to add anything to these shoes. The adhesive is just an extra step I like to take to ensure the design isn't going anywhere, since these shoes will likely be used for dancing and worn as keepsakes after the big day. The 3D flower in this photo came with the applique sent to me by the bride; however, a similar result can be achieved with embroidery stumpwork—an advanced embroidery technique.

Using a combination of lace and hand embroidery can result in a unique, stunning design that complements your wedding dress. I combined satin stitches with some delicate bridal lace and added some pearls to these shoes to match them to a bride's gown.

Alternate Shoelaces

Changing out standard shoelaces for organza or satin laces elevates the look. If you're planning to embroider a pair of laced sneakers for a special occasion like a wedding, switching the laces for a different material could be the perfect finishing touch. I find that white satin laces act like the final piece of a puzzle when working on bridal sneakers, but there are other laces that also work very well with wedding shoes. White organza laces are some of my favorites, and I often have brides who request these for more of a whimsical look. Many brides also like to add an element of blue on their shoes for their "something blue," which often happens to be the laces. I think this is an adorable way to honor this tradition and love nothing more than adding some light blue laces to a pair of hand-embroidered bridal sneakers.

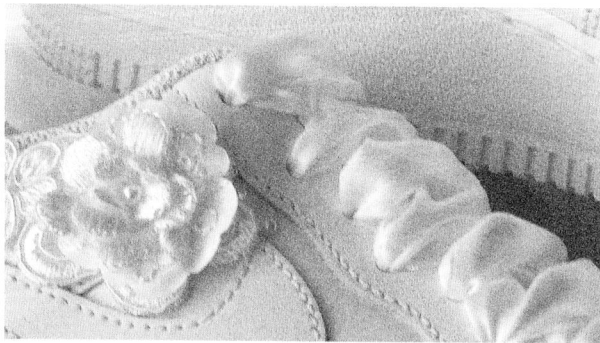

Try switching out the laces on your shoes with something more elegant.

PROJECT

Bridal Shoe Applique

This project is perfect if you have some lace or scraps from your wedding dress that you would like to add to your shoes. I'll walk you through how to customize your wedding shoes and create a timeless keepsake. Since the material you'll be working with will likely differ slightly from the material I've used for many of my bridal shoes, this tutorial will be less specific when it comes to the exact colors and stitches you should use.

I sewed an embroidered applique sent to me by a bride onto these shoes. I had to trim it to fit the shoe, and I added some straight stitches, pearls, and embroidered stumpwork petals to make the flowers more 3D. Stumpwork is an advanced embroidery technique and would be out of place in a beginner-friendly embroidery book, but I included this design to show you an example of an applique being trimmed down to fit the canvas of the shoe perfectly.

To achieve this result, I used a vintage piece of lace from a bride's grandmother's dress and added satin stitches in a matching thread color to make the design seem fuller. I used backstitches to sew the lace to the shoe and even managed to get the needle through the soles of the Converses, since they are not too thick, to secure the lace there.

BRIDAL SHOES 69

Color Guide

The colors you use for this project will depend on the color of the material you want to add to your shoes. Is it a bright white, or is it more of an ivory color? You can use the DMC thread color guide to match the material with a specific thread color. This is also a good time to choose other accent colors that might match your wedding color scheme. If you have pops of blue or small pink flowers in your bouquet, it might be a good idea to also add these onto your shoes.

Stitch Guide

The stitches you use for this project will depend on the fabric you're trying to attach to the shoes. You may decide that the material you want to use doesn't need extra stitches to embellish it. In this case, you can stitch it onto the shoe with small backstitches around the outer edges of the fabric. Take a look at the material: Are you using a delicate lace, or are there bold florals stitched onto the fabric? The key to creating a seamless bridal shoe design is incorporating lace with the perfect assortment of embroidery stitches to accompany it. When I am embroidering bridal shoes and using lace given to me by a client, I like to use stitches that resemble the lace or applique that I'm stitching on. I'll use a lot of satin stitches to create leaf shapes if there are similar stitches on the fabric, or a lot of French knots if there's more texture on the material. I work with the fabric to make the final result appear as cohesive as possible.

Measure and Cut the Material

Whether you are working with a cutting of lace or a ready-made embroidered applique, you will need to cut it down to size to fit the shoe you are working on. Analyze the fabric and see if there are any specific areas you think would look good on the inner or outer sides of the shoes. If you are working on shoes with a circular logo on the inner sides, take this into account—you don't want to cover this logo—it's best to work around the circle with smaller cuts of lace or applique. Measure both sides of your shoes before cutting your fabric of choice. Different shoe sizes will require different lengths of material to cover the desired area.

Using a Leather Hole Punch

If you are working on a pair of shoes that your embroidery needle can't get through, you may need to enlist the help of a leather punch. I recommend using a small-sized punch. You can use this leather punch to make small holes in your shoe wherever you want to attach the material. You can also use the leather punch in areas where you want to add your own stitches.

Using Glue

In some shoes, like Converse All Stars, the rubber soles that border the bottom of the shoes can easily be punctured with an embroidery needle. This may seem a little intimidating, but it's quite easy to do when wearing finger protectors. Other brands of shoes have thicker soles, which makes them almost impossible to embroider below the area where the fabric meets the rubber sole. If you are working on a pair of shoes with a thicker sole, you will need to use methyl methacrylate glue. This glue is an industrial adhesive and works perfectly with shoes because it's extremely strong. Anything you attach with this glue will be secure and won't come loose while wearing the shoes. I do not recommend using this glue on parts of the shoes that are made of canvas; it works best on rubber soles and very thick leather.

Chapter 7

Landscapes

In this chapter we'll learn techniques for some more-advanced embroidery projects. We've covered a whole host of stitches and floral embroidery patterns, but there are so many other things you can embroider onto your shoes! Landscapes and pets are some of the requests I get most often as a hand embroidery artist. First, in this chapter, I'll walk you through the process I use when embroidering landscapes.

Embroidering Landscapes

If there's a special place that comes to mind whenever you think of a picturesque landscape, then this might be the perfect project for you! I know that a specific location can hold some special memories, and this is just one way to create a keepsake for yourself or for someone special as a wonderful gift. This project would also work well for those who enjoy certain aspects of particular landscapes, like specific trees, flowers, or terrain.

If you plan to embroider a specific landscape onto your shoes, working from a photo might be the best way to ensure you capture all the details. Take a good look at the photo and pick out some particular things from the background and foreground. Are there mountains? If so, how many? Are there trees? A body of water? Perhaps you're embroidering a city skyline with varying heights of buildings.

Begin to mark out landmarks and important features in your digital sketching software or with a pencil and paper. The one thing to keep in mind when embroidering landscapes onto shoes is that there's not a lot of room to work with and you'll likely have to scale down the image you're working from. Keep in mind the stitches you've learned so far, and picture which ones would look good when embroidering certain elements in your landscape. It's helpful to make a note of this for later, when you're embroidering your design.

Once you've marked out specific landmarks in the background and foreground of the image, work on shading in some of the darker areas. This will make it easier to embroider the shadowed areas when it's time to stitch the landscape—and we want the finished product to look as realistic as possible. I would go as far as to say that if the mountains or trees don't have any shadows in the image you're working from, add some in!

The next step is to add in any smaller details that might make the scene more recognizable or more personal to you. If you're embroidering a spot that you visited with someone special, why not embroider both of you into the image? Adding two small human-like figures scaling the side of a mountain or sitting underneath a tree could be a sweet way to personalize these shoes even further. In this step, I like to add in any smaller bits of shrubbery and any wildlife I'd like to include. Changes in the terrain should be marked out here as well: Does it get rocky or grassy at a certain point? Make sure to note these changes in your sketch.

Even if you're not working from a photo of a specific landscape, the steps to achieving your finished design are the same. You'll still need to sketch out important aspects of your landscape, though you have more freedom to create something more custom. If you're just working from your own imagination, you can create a landscape filled with your favorite elements—the florals, colors, and terrain types are yours to create!

Once the sketch of your landscape is complete, it's time to transfer it to your shoes. Depending on which way you designed your pattern, you might be printing or sketching your design onto Fabri-Solvy paper, or just sketching it directly onto your shoes with an erasable marker.

Select your thread colors based on the colors in the image you're working from. Is it fall, spring, summer, or winter? Is the sun shining? Are the trees different colors of green? This is all very important and is probably the step that will take you the longest. Don't worry too much if this step becomes a little overwhelming. Keeping it simple is absolutely fine, and I lean toward oversimplifying my own landscape embroideries. I usually pick out three different colors for each of the components. For example, I'll choose three different shades of green for the trees and work from there.

Now it's time to get stitching! I always recommend starting with the larger design components first and working around those. If you have particularly large trees, mountains, or buildings in your landscape, stitch these first. If you made notes of which stitches you might like to use for certain components, now is a good time to check those notes.

> PROJECT

Mountains and Sunflowers

I created these shoes for a friend who loves to visit national parks. She travels to far too many for her to pick just one park to embroider onto a pair of shoes, so I created this design just for her. She loves mountains, sunflowers, and crescent moons—three elements I worked into the shoes. I added in some trees, stars, and greenery to tie the entire design together.

LANDSCAPES 73

Sketch Guide

Follow the sketch in figure 20 to replicate this exact design on the insides and outsides of your shoes with your erasable marker. This sketch is also a great size guide for how large each design component should be. Figure 21 shows a close-up of the design.

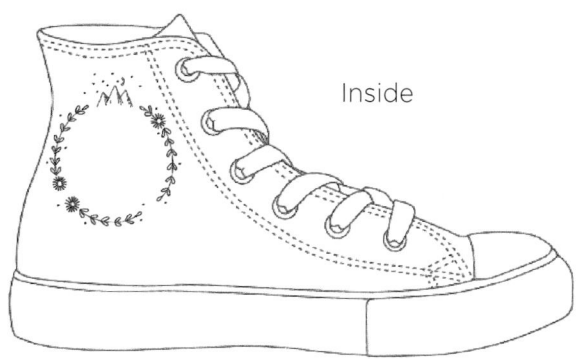 Inside  Outside

Figure 20

Figure 21

74 BEGINNER'S GUIDE TO SHOE EMBROIDERY

Basic Stitch and Thread Color Guide

We'll be going over these stitches and thread colors in more detail, but here are the basics for this design.

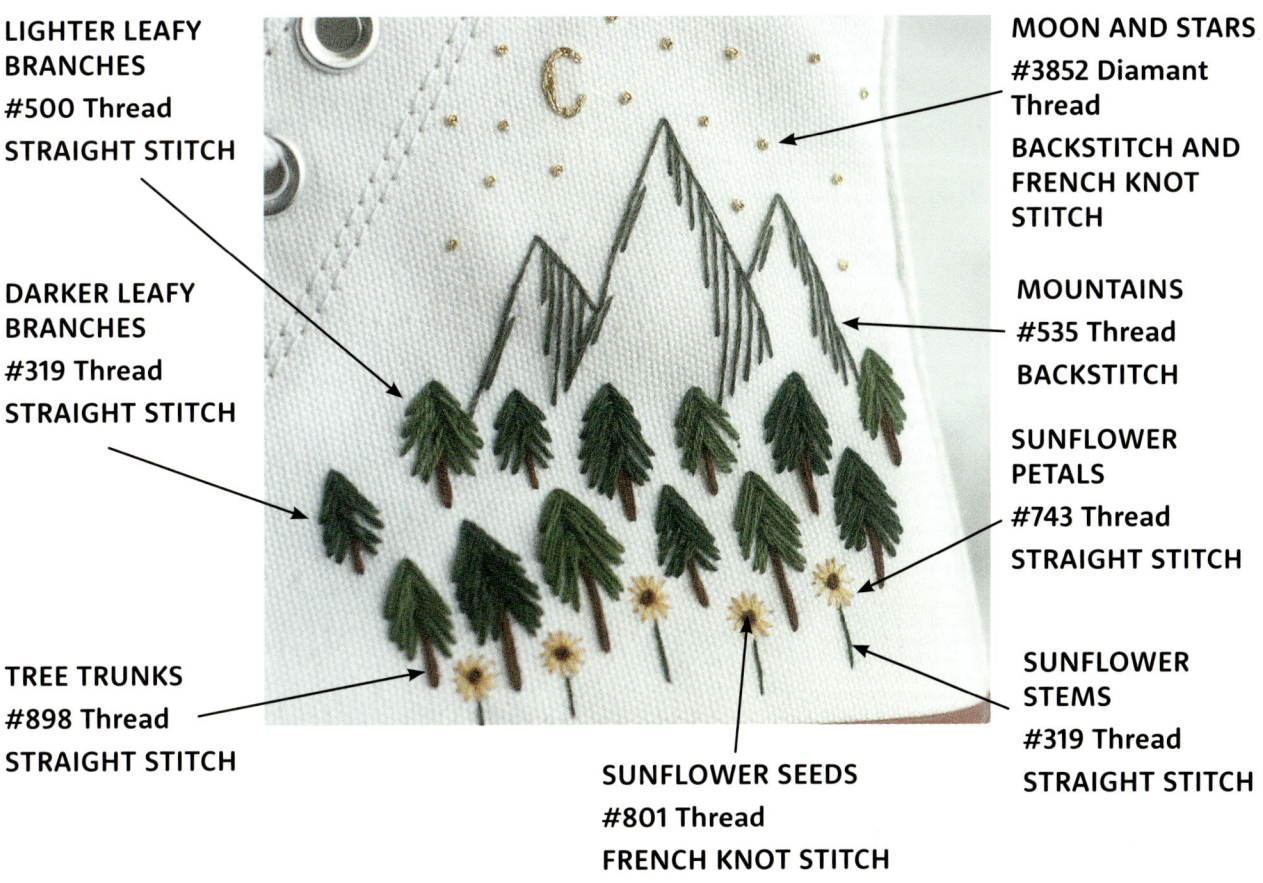

LIGHTER LEAFY BRANCHES
#500 Thread
STRAIGHT STITCH

DARKER LEAFY BRANCHES
#319 Thread
STRAIGHT STITCH

TREE TRUNKS
#898 Thread
STRAIGHT STITCH

MOON AND STARS
#3852 Diamant Thread
BACKSTITCH AND FRENCH KNOT STITCH

MOUNTAINS
#535 Thread
BACKSTITCH

SUNFLOWER PETALS
#743 Thread
STRAIGHT STITCH

SUNFLOWER STEMS
#319 Thread
STRAIGHT STITCH

SUNFLOWER SEEDS
#801 Thread
FRENCH KNOT STITCH

MOUNTAINS
#535 Thread
BACKSTITCH

SUNFLOWER SEEDS
#801 Thread
FRENCH KNOT STITCH

MOON AND STARS
#3852 Diamant Thread
BACKSTITCH AND FRENCH KNOT STITCH

SUNFLOWER PETALS
#743 Thread
STRAIGHT STITCH

STEM
#319 Thread
BACKSTITCH

LEAVES
#319 Thread
SATIN STITCH

LANDSCAPES

COLOR GUIDE

I stuck to more natural colors for this design to capture the essence of the landscape I pieced together. Using different hues of the same color can be a fantastic way to add dimension to a design that doesn't already have a lot of variation in color.

- #743 for the sunflower petals on both sides of the shoes
- #801 for the sunflower seeds on both sides of the shoes
- #535 for the mountains on both sides of the shoes
- #319 for the greenery stems and leaves on the insides of the shoes
- #3852 Diamant DMC Thread for the moon and stars on both sides of the shoes. This is a metallic thread we haven't used in any of the other projects. I recommend this thread when embroidering with metallic because it is the highest quality and the easiest to work with. You do not have to split this thread, just use the whole strand when stitching.
- #898 for the tree trunks on the outsides of the shoes
- #319 and #500 for the leafy branches on the outsides of the shoes
- #319 for the sunflower stems on the outsides of the shoes

Key Points

- We'll be using two strands of embroidery thread for the sunflower petals on the outsides of the shoes, four strands for the sunflower petals on the insides of the shoes, two strands for all the sunflower seeds, two strands for the greenery stems on the insides of the shoes, three strands for the leaves on the insides of the shoes, two strands for the mountains on the insides and outsides of the shoes, one strand for the moon and stars on the insides and outsides of the shoes, six strands for the tree trunks, four strands for the leafy branches, and two strands for the sunflower stems.
- We'll be using the straight stitch for the sunflower petals, the backstitch for the mountains, the backstitch for the greenery stems on the insides of the shoes, satin stitch for the leaves on the insides of the shoes, backstitch for the moon, French knots for the stars, French knots for the sunflower seeds, straight stitch for the leafy branches, and straight stitch for the sunflower stems.
- Remember to tie off and secure your thread inside the shoes after you complete each step. Loop your thread through some of the inner stitches two or three times before making at least two knots with your thread, then trim the excess thread.

Method for the Insides of the Shoes

1. Stitch the mountains with the backstitch:
    a. Thread your needle with two strands of #535 thread.
    b. Start at the bottom of one of the mountains and bring your needle up through the fabric.
    c. Make a ½-inch (1.25-cm) stitch following the line of the mountain outline; when you bring the needle back up through the fabric after that stitch, make sure to leave a ½-inch (1.25-cm) gap in the mountain outline.
    d. Fill the gap by stitching back up to the edge of the first stitch you made.
    e. Repeat this process until the mountain outlines are completely stitched, then use the same stitch for the terrain lines on the mountains.

BEGINNER'S GUIDE TO SHOE EMBROIDERY

2. Stitch the sunflower petals with the straight stitch:
   a. Thread your needle with four strands of #743 thread.
   b. Bring the needle up through the fabric at the outer edge of one of the sunflower petals.
   c. Bring it back down through the fabric at the opposite end of the petal. Repeat this stitch for the remaining eleven petals.
   d. Make sure to leave the center of the sunflowers empty—you'll be adding the seeds in here.
   e. Repeat this stitch for the remaining sunflowers.

3. Stitch the sunflower seeds with the French knot stitch:
   a. Thread your needle with two strands of #801 thread.
   b. Bring the needle up through the fabric in the center of the sunflower. Start at the edge and work around the circle in the center of the petals.
   c. Hold the needle with your non-dominant hand and loop your thread around your needle twice. Keep the needle pointed away from your work as you loop the thread around it.
   d. Position the needle as close as you can get to where it emerged originally, and bring it back down into the shoe fabric.
   e. Pull the thread through the fabric, keeping your thumb on top of the thread as it travels back through the fabric to control the knot.
   f. The knot should sit nicely on top of the fabric.
   g. Repeat this stitch until the center of the sunflower is filled with seeds. Repeat for the remaining sunflowers.

4. Stitch the greenery stems with the backstitch:
   a. Thread your needle with two strands of #319 thread.
   b. Bring the needle up through the fabric at the base of the first greenery stem. It doesn't matter which one you start with, just work around the circle from wherever you start.
   c. Make a ½-inch (1.25-cm) stitch down the stem before bringing the needle back up through the fabric ½ inch (1.25 cm) farther down from your initial stitch.
   d. Stitch backward, filling that ½-inch (1.25-cm) gap. Continue in this way until the stem is full.
   e. Repeat this stitch for the rest of the stems. Remember to follow the curve of the stems that you sketched out earlier.

5. Stitch the leaves with the satin stitch:
   a. Thread your needle with three strands of #319 thread.
   b. Bring your needle up through the fabric at the tip of one of the leaves you drew onto the stem. Again, it doesn't matter where you start, just work around the circle.
   c. Bring the needle back down through the fabric at the base of the leaf. Repeat this process, filling the entire surface area of the leaf as you stitch.
   d. Overlap your satin stitches for slightly puffier leaves.
   e. Create four or five satin stitches for each leaf.
   f. Repeat this process until all leaves are stitched.

6. Stitch the moon and stars with the backstitch and French knot stitch:
   a. Thread your needle with one strand of #3852 Diamant thread.
   b. For the moon: Bring your needle up through the fabric at the top of the moon.

LANDSCAPES 77

c. Make a tiny stitch along the curve of the moon. The shape is quite small, so the smaller the stitches the better.
d. Leave a tiny gap between your primary stitch and the next pass you make with the needle up through the fabric.
e. Stitch backward toward your first stitch, filling the gap you left with an equally tiny stitch.
f. Repeat this process with small backstitches until the crescent moon shape is full. Don't be afraid to overlap your stitches for a plumper shape.
g. For the stars: Bring the needle up through the fabric in the center of one of the circles you marked out for the stars. It doesn't matter where you start, but try to work from one side of the shoe to the other.
h. Hold the needle with your non-dominant hand and loop your thread around your needle twice. Keep the needle pointed away from your work as you loop the thread around it.
i. Position the needle as close as you can get to where it emerged originally, and bring it back down into the shoe fabric.
j. Pull the thread through the fabric, keeping your thumb on top of the thread as it travels back through the fabric to control the knot.
k. The knot should sit nicely on top of the fabric, like a perfect three-dimensional star.
l. Repeat this stitch until all the stars are stitched.

Method for the Outer Sides of the Shoes

1. Stitch the mountains with the backstitch:
   a. Thread your needle with two strands of #535 thread.
   b. Start at the bottom of one of the mountains and bring your needle up through the fabric.
   c. Make a ½-inch (1.25-cm) stitch following the line of the mountain outline; when you bring the needle back up through the fabric after that stitch, make sure to leave a ½-inch (1.25-cm) gap in the mountain outline.
   d. Fill the gap by stitching back up to the edge of the first stitch you made.
   e. Repeat this process until the mountain outlines are completely stitched, then use the same stitch for the terrain lines on the mountains.

2. Stitch the trunks of the trees with the straight stitch:
   a. Thread your needle with six strands of #898 thread.
   b. Bring the needle up through the fabric at the base of the first tree trunk. It doesn't matter which one you start with, but try to work from one side of the shoe to the other.
   c. Bring the needle back down through the fabric at the top of the tree trunk and pull your thread taut.
   d. Repeat this process for the rest of the tree trunks.

3. Stitch the leafy branches on the trees with the straight stitch:
   a. Thread one needle with four strands of #319 thread and another needle with four strands of #500 thread. Stitch half of the trees with #319 and the other half with #500.
   b. Bring your needle up through the fabric at the tip of your first leafy branch. It doesn't matter which one you start with, but I recommend starting with the branches on the top of the tree and working down the trunk.
   c. Bring your needle back down through the fabric at the apex point of the branch and pull your thread taut.

d. Repeat this process for the mirroring branch, and try to pull your thread back through the fabric in the same spot you pulled it through for the first branch. By overlapping the stitches slightly, the tree will come together nicely.

e. Repeat this process for all branches on each tree, and don't forget to switch colors between trees. Refer back to the finished photos of this design for exact color placements.

4. Stitch the sunflower petals with the straight stitch:
   a. Thread your needle with two strands of #743 thread.
   b. Bring the needle up through the fabric at the outer edge of one of the sunflower petals.
   c. Bring it back down through the fabric at the opposite end of the petal. Repeat this stitch for the remaining eleven petals.
   d. Make sure to leave the center of the sunflowers empty—you'll be adding the seeds in here.
   e. Repeat this stitch for your remaining sunflowers.

5. Stitch the sunflower seeds with the French knot stitch:
   a. Thread your needle with two strands of #801 thread.
   b. Bring the needle up through the fabric in the center of the sunflower—you're just stitching one seed in the center of these sunflowers since they are much smaller.
   c. Hold the needle with your non-dominant hand and loop your thread around your needle twice. Keep the needle pointed away from your work as you loop the thread around it.
   d. Position the needle as close as you can get to where it emerged originally, and bring it back down into the shoe fabric.
   e. Pull the thread through the fabric, keeping your thumb on top of the thread as it travels back through the fabric to control the knot.
   f. The knot should sit nicely on top of the fabric.
   g. Repeat this stitch in the center of the remaining sunflowers.

6. Stitch the stem of the sunflowers with the straight stitch:
   a. Thread your needle with two strands of #319 thread.
   b. Bring your needle up through the fabric at the base of the stem.
   c. Bring the needle back down through the fabric at the top of the stem where it connects with the sunflower head and pull your thread taut.
   d. Repeat this process for the rest of the sunflower stems.

7. Stitch the moon and stars with the backstitch and French knot stitch:
   a. Thread your needle with one strand of #3852 Diamant thread.
   b. For the moon: Bring your needle up through the fabric at the top of the moon.
   c. Make a tiny stitch along the curve of the moon. The shape is quite small, so the smaller the stitches the better.
   d. Leave a tiny gap between your primary stitch and the next pass you make with the needle up through the fabric.
   e. Stitch backward toward your first stitch, filling the gap you left with an equally tiny stitch.
   f. Repeat this process with small backstitches until the crescent moon shape is full. Do not be afraid to overlap your stitches for a plumper shape.
   g. For the stars: Bring the needle up through the fabric in the center of one of the circles you marked out for the stars. It doesn't matter where you start, but try to work from one side of the shoe to the other.

h. Hold the needle with your non-dominant hand and loop your thread around your needle twice. Keep the needle pointed away from your work as you loop the thread around it.

i. Position the needle as close as you can get to where it emerged originally, and bring it back down into the shoe fabric.

j. Pull the thread through the fabric, keeping your thumb on top of the thread as it travels back through the fabric to control the knot.

k. The knot should sit nicely on top of the fabric, like a perfect three-dimensional star.

l. Repeat this stitch until all the stars are stitched.

TIPS

- Working with metallic thread is a little more challenging than regular embroidery thread because it is more prone to snagging and knotting. Work slowly and methodically when stitching your moon and stars for this design. If you are really struggling, you can swap out the metallic thread for #976 thread, which is not metallic but golden in color.
- You can add in extra straight stitches for your leafy branches if your trees are looking a bit bare! I will sometimes go in and add a few extra branches here and there to fluff them up a little.
- Don't forget to stitch the stars that are polka-dotted in the circle on the inner sides of the shoes. It's easy to miss them, but they are a key component in bringing this design together.

Chapter 8

Pets

I find myself embroidering two or three pairs of pet sneakers every single week, which leads me to believe that this may be one of the most highly anticipated sections of this book! As someone who owns a dog and a cat, I can absolutely understand the love that my embroidered pet shoes receive. Many brides like to wear pet sneakers on their big days to have their fur-babies be a part of their weddings—which is something I wholeheartedly love and support. But pet embroidery is by far one of the most challenging projects we'll be tackling in this book. Since I can't give you a detailed guide on how to specifically embroider your own pet, I will go through the steps to design and complete this project on your own. I'll also show you how I embroider my own pets, to give you more of a visual guide for your own pet embroidery projects.

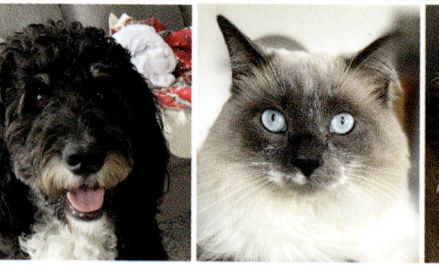

First, you'll need a photo of your pet. You can embroider your dog, cat, bird, horse, lizard—the list is endless and there are no limitations. Just try to make sure they're facing the camera so you have a good shot of their facial features and head shape. Natural lighting is also best so that you can choose thread colors based on their coloring.

You'll need to sketch an outline of your pet's head and shoulders. I stick to embroidering pets from their chest up; this makes it easier to focus on their facial features and to nail their likeness rather than spending lots of time embroidering their limbs and such. If you have ProCreate, you can trace around your pet's photo and get an exact outline of their head and facial features. If you don't use digital sketching software, you can do this on a piece of paper. Alternatively, you can take your erasable marker and start outlining your pet's head and features directly onto the shoe. Since I have been doing this for years, I sketch directly onto the shoes when embroidering pets, but I do recommend that first-timers take some time to sketch out the outline of their pet's heads and facial features before transferring the design onto the shoes.

Following are some tips for sketching and embroidering the pets I embroider the most.

A good pet photo will capture the animal's facial features and head shape.

Dogs

- Different breeds of dogs have different head shapes. Bully breeds tend to have larger, blockier heads, which I find much easier to sketch out usually. Smaller dogs like chihuahuas and terriers tend to have narrower faces and smaller features, which means you may need to pay closer attention when sketching them onto your shoes.

82 BEGINNER'S GUIDE TO SHOE EMBROIDERY

Pay close attention to the shape and positioning of the dog's ears. For shepherds, the upright pointy ears are a key characteristic.

Each dog will have unique color variations in their fur that you will want to replicate with your thread selections.

- Start with the general shape of the head and then move on to adding the ears (figure 22). Pay attention to the ears: Do they hang on either side of the face? Do they stick up in the air? Make sure to get the proportions right when adding the ears onto the head shape.
- Once you've sketched out the head and ears, it's time to add the facial features (figure 23). This does not have to be super detailed. I usually start with the nose, which is typically somewhere around the center of the face, and work from there to add in both eyes. For the nose and eyes, I just draw a rough shape—no need to add in any details since we will be embroidering over the sketches and can add details later.

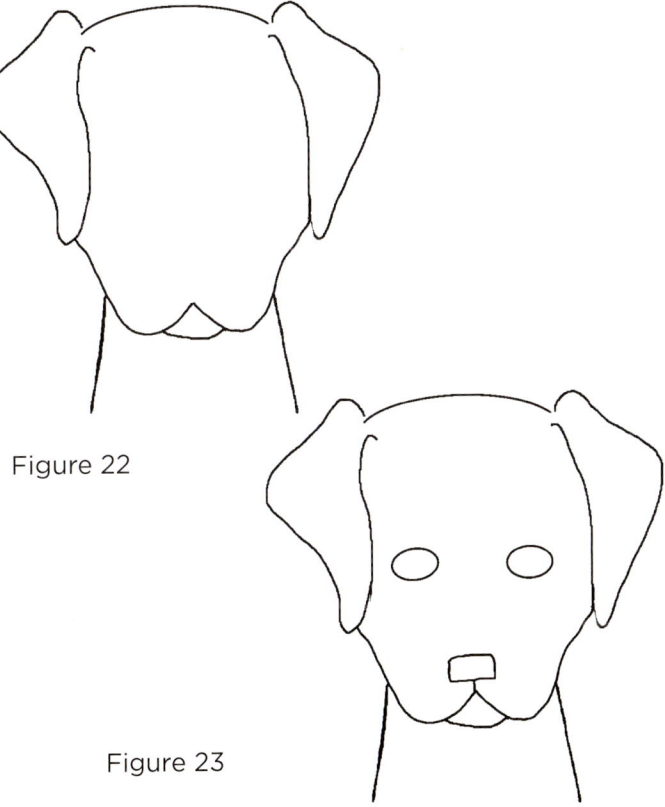

Figure 22

Figure 23

- If your dog has any specific markings like eyebrows, a white stripe up their face, or spots of different-colored fur, mark this out in your sketch (figure 24). This will be a reminder to change thread colors for that specific area. It doesn't have to be extremely neat—remember we will be embroidering over those lines. Depending on the length of your dog's coat, you may need to mark out particularly fluffy areas when sketching.
- To finish up your sketch, mark out the grain direction of your dog's fur with some lines across their face (figure 25). This will make it easier to embroider each section of your dog's face.

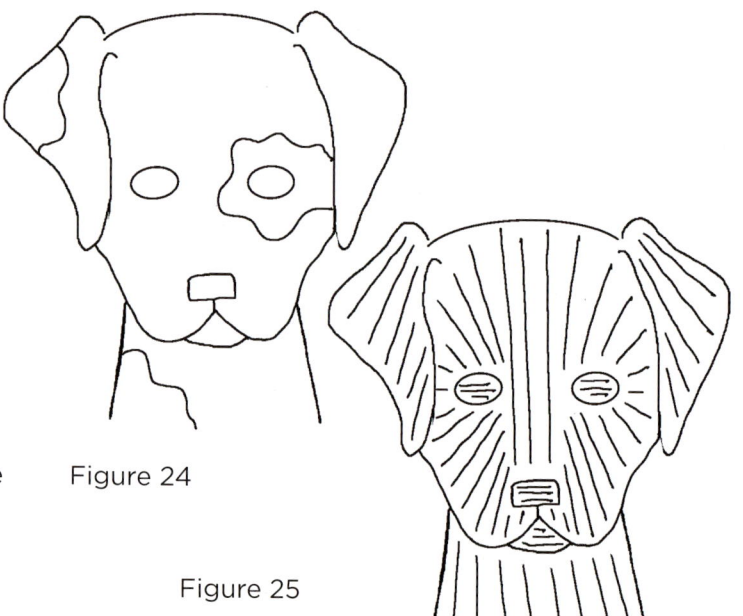

Figure 24

Figure 25

Cats

Most cats have similar facial features; therefore, getting their coloring just right is very important in personalizing your embroidery.

- Unlike dogs, most cats I have embroidered seem to have very similar facial structures (figure 26). Unless you have a specific breed like a Maine coon or a Sphynx cat, your cat should have quite a round/oval face. Mark out the shape of your cat's face before adding the ears. The ears of most cats tend to be triangular, and they're quite easy to mark out on the tops of their heads. I often embroider cats that have a little chunk missing from one of their ears—or in some cases an entire ear missing! Don't forget to add these little details into your own sketches.

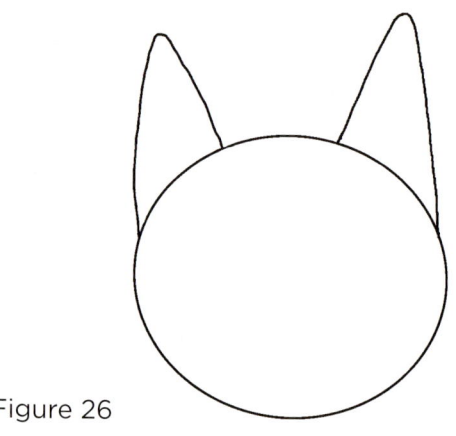

Figure 26

84 BEGINNER'S GUIDE TO SHOE EMBROIDERY

- Next, add your cat's nose (figure 27). Depending on the photo you're working from, the nose usually sits a little under the middle of your cat's face. From here, you can add in your cat's eyes. These don't need to be super detailed; they're mainly for placement purposes as we'll be adding in the details when we embroider.
- If your cat has any specific markings like a nose stripe or spots on their face, mark these out (figure 28). This will be a reminder for you to change thread color when embroidering.
- If your cat has longer hair, make sure to include this in your sketch (figure 29). The longhaired cats I have embroidered tend to be bushier from their ears to their chests, which means you'll need to embroider more hair around their faces. You can also mark out the cat's whiskers here, but remember that we'll be embroidering over most of these marks before adding the whiskers (figure 30). I usually just stitch the whiskers on at the very end of the embroidery project since they sit on top of the cat's cheeks.
- To finish out the sketch of your cat, mark out the grain direction of your cat's fur with some lines across their face and chest (figure 31). This will make it easier to embroider each section of your cat's face.
- While I'm unable to walk you through a pet embroidery pattern for your specific pet, I hope these instructions can assist you in embroidering your furry friend onto some sneakers!

The embroidery portion of this project is surprisingly simple. I stick with the satin stitch to embroider most of the body, making sure to stitch in the same direction the fur appears to grow in. I use one single strand of embroidery thread—this is important. By using one strand of thread, it gives the effect of hairs, and it makes it easy to add in small details like tufts of fur.

To find the perfect color match for your pet, take their photo and compare it to the DMC

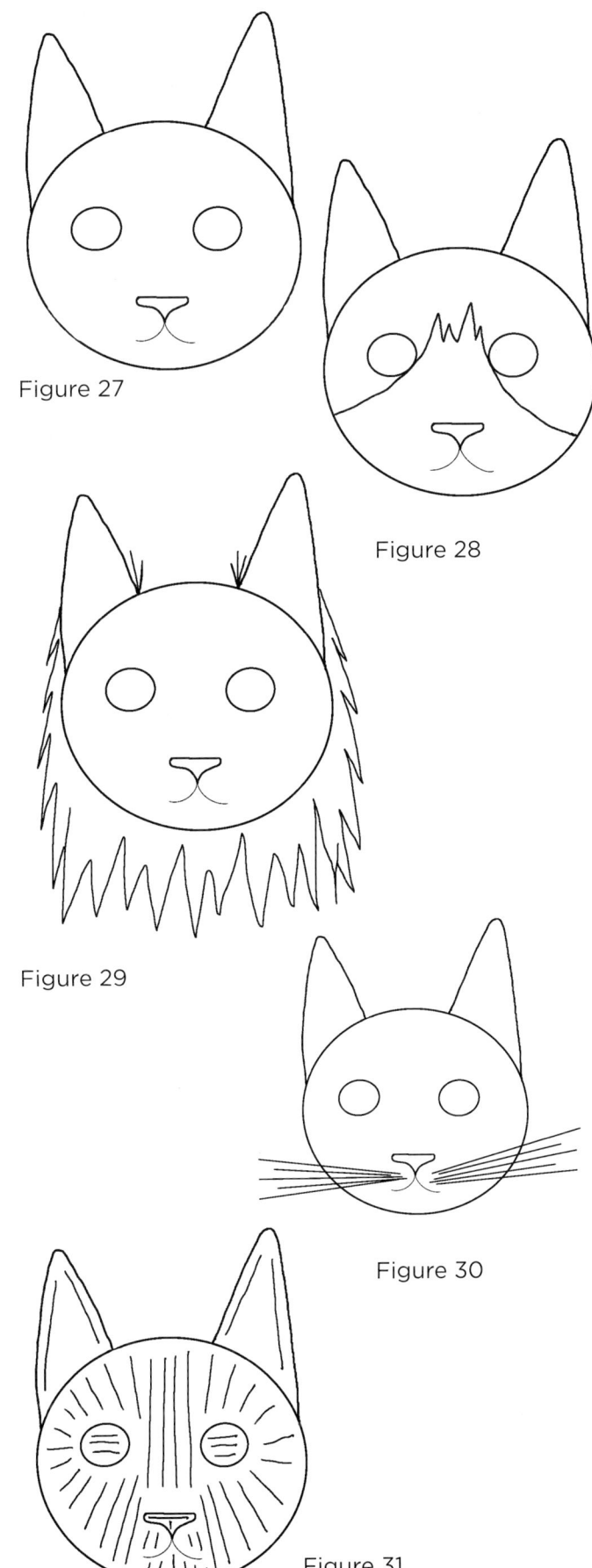

Figure 27

Figure 28

Figure 29

Figure 30

Figure 31

color chart online. You might find that you need to experiment with different color combinations and see which ones complement each other in a way that resembles your pet's fur.

As I promised earlier, I'll now take you through my pet embroidery process with portraits of my own pets.

TIPS

A summary of my top tips for pet embroidery:
- Lots of small, dainty stitches will result in a realistic end product.
- Don't be afraid to use a spectrum of different colors. Even if your pet is only one color, they likely have different shades of fur all over their face.
- Don't rush the smaller details like the nose and eyes. These are the features of your pet that make them recognizable. Make sure you get the perfect eye color and capture any of the smaller details like whether the whites of their eyes usually show or if their nose is made up of a couple of different colors.
- Remember all the stitches and tips you've learned throughout this book. Tying off and securing your thread between color changes is important, as always.

PROJECT

Dave the Cat

Dave is an eight-year-old American shorthair cat, and he loves to pose for the camera! He's mostly orange with some white markings on his face, so I made sure to outline those markings in my initial sketch on the shoes. This initial sketch doesn't have to be super detailed, since we will be embroidering over all of these markings, but I do take my time to make sure that I get the right proportions for his eyes, nose, and ears. I used a fine-line pencil to gently sketch out his face onto the shoes, but you can use an erasable embroidery marker if you're worried you might make a mistake. Alternatively, you could trace around an image of your cat's face using digital drawing software and print their likeness onto some Fabri-Solvy paper, but not everyone has access to this paper and the specific printer it requires, so I'm showing you how to embroider your pet by directly sketching onto your shoes.

My reference photo of Dave.

My first sketch of Dave on the shoe.

My finished embroidery of Dave.

PETS 87

Basic Stitch and Thread Color Guide

For this project, we'll only need to use satin stitches and a small number of straight stitches and backstitches. The thread colors you'll need to embroider your pet will likely differ from these, but to embroider Dave I used six different thread colors:

- #3853 for the majority of his face and ears
- #3852 for his eyes
- #5200 for the white accents on his face, the white hairs in his ears, and his whiskers
- #310 to define his eyes and his mouth, and for his pupils
- #3064 for the darker orange accents on his face
- #3716 for the insides of his ears and for his nose

Key Points

- We'll be using one strand of embroidery thread for this entire project.
- Remember to tie off and secure your thread inside the shoes after you complete each step. Loop your thread through some of the inner stitches two or three times before making at least two knots with your thread, then trim the excess thread.

Method

1. Stitch the fur on the face and outer edges of the ears with the satin stitch:
    a. Thread your needle with one strand of #3853. It's always best to start with the color that will cover most of the pet's face.
    b. Start near the center of the pet's face and bring the needle up through the fabric.
    c. Insert your needle back into the fabric at the border of the sketch. Remember to stitch in the direction of the pet's hair growth. Pay close attention to your sketch—don't stitch over the lines that mark out the different-colored accents on the face.
    d. To stitch the ears, start at the base of each, and stitch upward using the straight stitch, working your way around and back down toward the face once you're done with one side. Keep the borders of the ears thin, and leave the inner ears bare of thread.

2. Stich the insides of the ears with the satin stitch:
    a. Thread your needle with one strand of #3716.
    b. Start at the base of the ears and bring the needle up through the fabric.
    c. Bring the needle down through the fabric inside the orange borders of the ears, stitching directly upward.
    d. Repeat this stitch, keeping your stitches parallel as you work to fill the ears with thread.

3. Stitch the remaining fur on the face with the satin stitch:
   a. Thread your needle with one strand of #5200.
   b. Bring your needle up through the fabric just above the nose.
   c. Bring it back down at the apex of the nose stripe.
   d. Repeat this stitch until the nose stripe is stitched before continuing with the satin stitch on other areas of the face. Remember to work in the direction that the hair grows.

5. Stitch the irises of the eyes with the satin stitch:
   a. Thread your needle with one strand of #3852.
   b. Bring your needle up through the fabric on the far-left side of one eye.
   c. Insert the needle back into the fabric on the far-right side of the eye—it's best to make this initial stitch in the center of the eye and work outward from the first stitch.
   d. Repeat this process until the eye is filled with satin stitch. You can overlap these stitches to make the eyes stand out a little from the rest of the face.
   e. Don't forget to stitch the other eye with the same technique!

4. Stitch the borders around the eyes with the backstitch:
   a. Thread your needle with one strand of #310.
   b. Bring your needle up through the fabric at the base of one of the eyes. The eyes should be empty of thread.
   c. Insert your needle back down into the fabric a short distance away from where you brought it up through the fabric, following the border of the eye.
   d. Repeat this stitch until the borders are lined with a thin line of black thread. Make sure to do this for both eyes!

6. Stitch the accents onto the face with satin stitches and straight stitches:
   a. Thread your needle with one strand of #3064 for the darker orange stripes on the face.
   b. Bring your needle up through the fabric at the base of one of the darker stripes. You will be working directly from a photo of the pet for this step since these details are being added on top of fur we have already stitched.

c. Bring your needle back down through the fabric at the end of the darker stripe.
d. Repeat this process for all of the darker orange stripes on the pet's face until they are filled with straight stitches.
e. Thread your need with one strand of #3716.
f. Bring your needle up through the fabric at far-left side of the nose.
g. Bring your needle back down through the fabric on the far-right side of the nose.
h. Repeat this process, following the tapering shape of the nose until it is filled with satin stitch.
i. Thread your needle with one strand of #5200.
j. Bring your needle up through the fabric underneath the nose, at the base of the whisker. You will be working directly from an image of the pet for the whiskers.
k. Insert your needle back into the fabric at the end of the whisker, making sure to extend each whisker past the border of the pet's face.
l. Repeat this straight stitch for all of the whiskers.
m. Use the one strand of #5200 for more straight stitches inside the pet's ears, starting at the base of the ear and working your way upward.
n. Continue with the #5200 for one tiny straight stitch in the corner of each eye, to emulate a glint in both eyes.
o. Thread your needle with one strand of #310.
p. Bring it up through the center of one of the eyes, closer to the base than the top, and stitch upward.
q. Repeat this process until the desired pupil size is achieved. Remember to add pupils to both eyes.

TIPS

- Pay close attention to your pet's whiskers. Do they droop or stick straight out from their face? Do they have any whiskers growing from their eyebrows?
- The more colors you use, the easier it will be to capture your pet's likeness. If you have a darker-colored pet, this will be crucial to achieving a realistic embroidered portrait. Choose different hues of the same color and make sure you pay close attention to the reference photo.
- If your pet wears a specific accessory, don't be afraid to embroider them with it! A collar or a bow can be a super fun addition to a pet embroidery project.

PROJECT

Lio the Dog

Lio is an eight-year-old border collie/blue heeler mix who *also* enjoys posing for a photo! Lio has a very unique fur pattern, which makes for an interesting embroidery project. He also has longer fur than some other breeds, which translates well into the medium of embroidery. I will be showing you how to complete this project using the sketching method again.

My reference photo of Lio.

My sketch of Lio on the shoe.

My finished embroidery of Lio.

PETS

Basic Stitch and Thread Color Guide

For this project, we'll only need to use satin stitches and a small number of straight stitches. The thread colors you choose to embroider your pet will likely differ from these, but to embroider Lio I used three different thread colors.

- #5200 for the majority of his face and neck
- #310 for his left ear, nose, eyes, and accent spots on his face and neck
- #975 for the remaining accent dots on his face and neck

Key Points

- We'll be using one strand of embroidery thread for this entire project.
- Remember to tie off and secure your thread inside the shoes after you complete each step. Loop your thread through some of the inner stitches two or three times before making at least two knots with your thread, then trim the excess thread.

Method

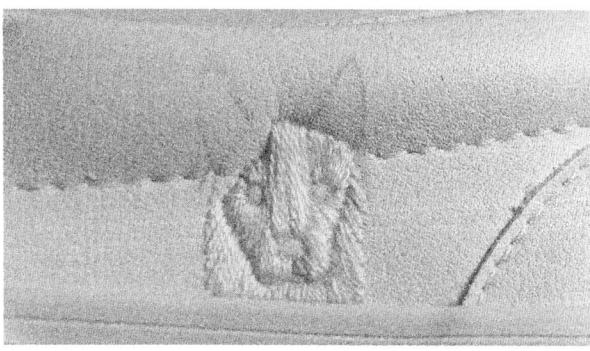

1. Stitch the fur on the face with the satin stitch:
    a. Thread your needle with one strand of #5200.
    b. Bring your needle up through the fabric in the center of the pet's face, just above the nose.
    c. Stitch upward, inserting the needle back into the fabric at the apex of the pet's head.
    d. Repeat this stitch, filling the face of the pet with satin stitch. Remember to follow the outlines of the accents that you need to fill with a different color, and stitch in the same direction that the fur grows.

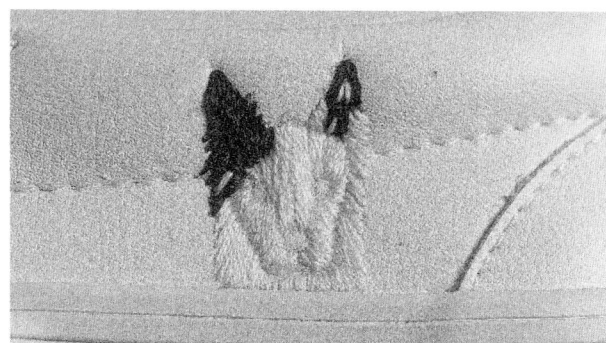

2. Stitch the black left ear and the black sections on the right ear:
    a. Thread your needle with one strand of #310.
    b. Insert your needle at the base of the left ear.
    c. Mimic the hairs on the ears by inserting the needle back into the fabric a small distance away from where you brought it up through the fabric.
    d. The tops of the ears are smoother, with less wispy hairs, so direct your satin stitches accordingly.
    e. Remember to stitch the black accents on the right ear by following the direction of hair growth and stitching them among the white hairs of the ear.

3. Stitch the accents and remaining features on the face with satin stitches and straight stitches:
   a. Thread your needle with one strand of #310.
   b. Bring your needle up through the shoe fabric on the far-left side of the nose, which should be bare of thread.
   c. Bring your needle back through the fabric on the far-right side of the nose. It's best to make this initial stitch in the center of the nose, almost cutting it in half with the first stitch, because then you can work from that stitch and keep the rest of your stitches parallel as you fill the nose with satin stitches.
   d. Repeat this process for the eyes, filling them with satin stitches and tapering the edges to fill the shapes we sketched earlier.
   e. For the accent spots on the pet's face, make small straight stitches with one strand of #310 and #975.
   f. Repeat these small straight stitches until all of the accents on the pet's face are stitched—don't forget about the neck and ears.

TIPS

- If your pet often sticks their tongue out for photos, don't be afraid to embroider this in their portrait!
- To commemorate lost pets, consider adding a halo, stitched in gold or silver, above their heads in their embroidered portraits.
- Add an arrangement of florals and greenery around the base of your pet's neck to make these the perfect wedding shoes!

Chapter 9

Care and Maintenance

If you put hours, maybe even days, into a shoe embroidery project, you will want to make sure your embroidery lasts. It's crucial to follow the instructions listed for each embroidery project by tying off and securing your thread meticulously after you complete each section of the design you're working on. Additionally, there are a few things to note when it comes to the care and maintenance of your embroidered shoes or boots.

Always wear socks when sporting your embroidered footwear; the embroidery doesn't need backing or any special care other than a pair of socks to create a barrier between your skin and the stitches. Wearing socks prevents the natural oils in your skin from making contact with the embroidery and wearing it down. If you're planning on wearing your creations regularly and you want the embroidery to last, put your socks on! I own and wear several pairs of hand-embroidered sneakers and boots, and I can't feel any of the stitches when wearing my embroidered footwear, even my more intricate designs. Embroidery thread is far hardier than it looks, and if you secure your thread as per the project instructions, your embroidery will last for decades.

If you're anticipating wet weather when wearing your embroidered footwear, you may want to waterproof them with a spray that will make it easier to remove mud and dirt from the shoes. The spray you need will depend on the fabric of the shoes; for example, if you embroidered onto a pair of canvas sneakers, you'll need to purchase some waterproof spray for canvas sneakers. There are a few sprays I recommend, and I have listed them in Suppliers on page 104.

One of the questions I get asked the most involves embroidered shoes and washing machines, and I can't emphasize this enough—please do not throw your embroidered sneakers or boots in the washing machine! You shouldn't wash any structured canvas sneakers this way, although I've heard that it's a common method. Athletic shoes, maybe, but canvas sneakers and leather boots are not designed to be washed in a washing machine.

Spot cleaning is best for your hand-embroidered shoes.

Doing so can and will affect the structural integrity of the footwear, which is less than ideal, especially if you just spent hours embroidering them!

To clean your hand-embroidered footwear, I recommend spot cleaning with uncolored detergent and a microfiber towel. The embroidery thread I recommend in this book is high quality, and I have never experienced color leaching from this thread to discolor the shoe, but if you're working with a different brand of embroidery thread, be careful of this. By using a small amount of detergent, some warm water, and a microfiber towel, you can gently cleanse the soiled areas on the shoes. I never recommend submerging the entire shoe or boot in water; spot cleaning is the safest way to clean your shoes and make sure they last as long as possible.

Photographing and Sharing Your Finished Projects

Photography

There are several things to consider when photographing your work. These include but are not limited to:
- The equipment you use to take the photographs
- The background
- The lighting

EQUIPMENT

When it comes to photography equipment, you don't need to go and invest hundreds of dollars on a camera if you already have a decent smartphone. Most phones have high-quality cameras these days, and by toggling the settings a little, it's easy for your photos to showcase the effort you put into your embroidery.

I take my photos with a Canon Rebel XTI, one of their older DSLR models. I spent a little extra money on a 50-mm lens to help me capture more up-close shots of my embroidery. I got this camera secondhand for just over $100 seven years ago, but I use it almost every day when taking photos of my work. If you have a little extra cash to invest in a camera, I recommend doing some research and buying a highly rated piece of equipment that will serve your needs. Lenses are often far more important in taking the kinds of photos you want. I knew I wanted my photos to show my work in great detail. It was also important that my photos looked professional because I use photos of my hand-embroidered shoes when marketing my products.

After doing some deep dives into camera forums, I discovered I could get the photos I wanted with an older camera body—like the Canon Rebel XTI that I now own—but I would need a different lens than the standard one the camera came with. If there's a specific look you're wanting to achieve with your own photographs, you may need to research the kind of setup that will work for you.

BACKGROUND

It's always important to consider the background and setup of your photos before you start snapping away. There are all kinds of software that allow you to remove the backgrounds

This photo has a distracting background and bad lighting. It was taken in front of a window with harsh light coming in and a random windowpane visible in the background.

Good background example: simple background, one color. It contrasts with the color of the shoes, which makes them the focus of the photo.

of your images and edit your photos to look the way you want them to, but it's easy to avoid doing all this if you put in a little effort.

I like to keep things simple when I'm taking photos of my shoes. I often use the same backdrop because I think keeping my aesthetic consistent helps build my brand on social media. I have a 60-inch (152.5-cm) rectangle of white satin fabric that I place on a table or the floor in front of a natural source of light. If I want to take photos of the shoes from a different angle, I'll prop the fabric up and make sure that the only thing in the background is the white satin. With my camera equipment, the lens will often blur out the background of my photos—called a bokeh effect—and I love the way it looks when I can achieve this with the simple background I often use.

When taking photos of your own embroidery projects, I recommend using a simple background. You don't have to buy a sheet of fabric for this; using a wall or a relatively plain corner in your home will work just as well. You want to make sure the focus of your photos is the shoes and the embroidery you've spent so long completing. Taking photos of them in a busy environment with a bunch of other colors and things going on in the photo will distract from your hard work.

LIGHTING

Lighting is often a hot topic of discussion among people who enjoy photography, but my opinion is that natural lighting will always trump artificial lighting. As someone who works as an embroidery artist throughout the year, the winter months can be challenging when shooting content because of the limited amount of daylight. For this reason, I have some box lights in my studio that are supposed to replicate light from the sun, but, when I'm editing, I can always tell which photos were taken under these artificial lights.

Taking photos in natural light will make the editing process much easier, and your embroidery projects will look much clearer in the photos. I like to set my shoes in front of a window, not in any direct rays of sun but in a spot where the light illuminates the shoes and shows off the stitching. Natural lighting will also showcase the colors of the threads in a realistic way that usually can't be replicated in editing when trying to fix photos taken under artificial light.

Sharing on Social Media

Social media can be a fantastic place to share your finished crafts and discover a community of like-minded artists. The three platforms I recommend for sharing your embroidery projects are:
- Instagram
- TikTok
- YouTube

INSTAGRAM

I love sharing my work on Instagram because the platform is so diverse. I have met so many different people on the app, many of whom share my love for embroidery. Social media algorithms change quite often, so while there isn't a surefire way to get your art pushed out to other creatives, there are a couple of things you can try when sharing your art. Using hashtags and trending sounds can often give your posts a boost in views. Doing this consistently will pay off, as will posting as often as possible. Try to use all different forms of posting on Instagram: Stories, reels, and carousel posts will perform differently but often reach different demographics on the app. Interacting with other posts from people who also enjoy embroidery is a fantastic way to make friends within the hand embroidery community.

TIKTOK

This video-sharing app is a little different from Instagram and has its own algorithms and challenges. TikTok is an app that focuses on short-form content but often pushes out videos that are over sixty seconds, even rewarding creators for making videos that are over a minute long. One way to get your art seen on TikTok and

This is an example of bad lighting. Light and shadows coming in through blinds obscure the design on the shoes.

Good lighting is even across the photo and showcases the design in the foreground and background.

grow your community is by being authentic and showing your process as an artist. I have seen others find success in sharing stories about their art and experiences with certain mediums. Storytelling is the easiest way to connect with others on TikTok, so if you're good at having conversations and talking to the camera, this app might be the perfect place for you to build an audience.

YOUTUBE

Long-form content is often the most difficult to plan and create, so it's no wonder that a lot of people are intimidated by YouTube. The good news is that YouTube shorts are perfect for shorter-form content that you can also post on both Instagram and TikTok if you're not ready to branch out into long-form content. Filming longer videos and taking more time to engage with other artists and people who enjoy watching your content are great ways to build a solid community. I love following other creatives on YouTube because there's a level of connection that comes along with watching someone film an entire art vlog. Embroidery is a fantastic artform to share on a platform like YouTube because it's a time-consuming process, and one that a lot of people want to learn and appreciate.

CONCLUSION

I truly hope that you've found some inspiration within the pages of this book. Perhaps you plan to try your hand at one of my shoe embroidery patterns, and if that is the case, please share your embroidered shoes with me! You can find me @HanEmbroiders on all social media platforms, and I'd love nothing more than to see your creations.

Hand embroidery is such a special craft, one that I hold close to my heart. It's my hope that this book has given you the tools you need to begin your own hand embroidery projects, perhaps even design your own shoe embroidery patterns! Whether you're crafting for yourself, making gifts for loved ones, or even considering a new business venture, each project is a step toward honing your skills and unleashing your artistic potential.

Thank you so much for joining me on this journey of shoes and stitches. I appreciate your readership and support more than you know.

ACKNOWLEDGMENTS

Writing an extensive craft book was not something I had on my to-do list for 2024. I have always loved to write, always loved to teach, and always loved to embroider—so writing this book has been an absolute dream. Thank you so much to Candi Derr and the team at Stackpole Books for working with me on this project. I appreciate you and all of your hard work.

Learning the craft of hand embroidery at such a young age allowed me to continue the craft through the past twenty years, stitching whenever I had the time and eventually creating a business around it. To my dearest Nanna, the woman who put a needle and thread in my hand at age seven, thank you for teaching me everything you knew. This book would never have been possible without you. I miss you with every fiber of my being, and I know you would have been the first one to snatch this book off the shelves.

To my incredible husband, Kenyon, your unwavering support and love have been so crucial in my embarking on this journey and writing a book about the craft I love. From listening to my endless embroidery ramblings to the nights when I stitched shoes until the sun came up, you've been a rock throughout, and I couldn't ask for a better partner.

And to you, the reader, thank you again for your support. I hope to see many of your embroidery projects, and I look forward to hearing your feedback and connecting with you all on social media!

GLOSSARY

Backstitch: A type of stitch where the needle goes backward from the direction of the sewing, often used for outlining.

Bobbin: A spool or cylinder around which thread or yarn is wound.

Couch stitch: A type of stitch that you use for longer stems in which, rather than making lots of individual stitches, you make one long stitch and anchor it to the fabric at certain points with smaller stitches.

Embroidery marker: Erasable marker that can be removed after stitching is complete.

Fabri-Solvy paper: Sticky paper stabilizer you can print or sketch your design onto before placing it onto your shoes for stitching. Remove with water.

Finger protectors: Thimbles for the tips of your fingers to protect your skin and make it easier to pull the needle through the fabric.

Floss: Embroidery thread, typically made of cotton, and composed of six strands that can be separated.

French knot stitch: A decorative knot made by wrapping thread around the needle and pulling it through the fabric, creating a small bump.

Lazy daisy stitch: A stitch made by securing a small loop of thread to the fabric, used most often for petals or leaves.

Satin stitch: A stitch used to fill areas with a smooth and glossy appearance, created by closely placed stitches.

Stabilizer: Material placed under fabric to prevent shifting or stretching during embroidery, ensuring a neat finish. It is not typically necessary in shoe embroidery.

Straight stitch: A stitch used to create a simple, straight line in a petal or blade of grass.

Thread tension: The tightness of the thread, crucial for creating even and consistent stitches.

SUPPLIERS

In this section, I'll give you the details of where I source the materials and supplies I use in my shoe embroidery projects. Many of the supplies listed in this book can be purchased from a craft store, but I order a lot of my supplies online due to the convenience and the ability to buy in bulk.

I do not recommend buying branded shoes from unverified retailers, particularly if shopping online, to avoid accidentally purchasing fake shoes.

Hand Embroidery Tools

AMAZON
www.amazon.com
Provides all supplies necessary for shoe embroidery: needles, scissors, thread, Fabri-Solvy paper, finger protectors, Crep Protect shoe protector spray, Kiwi shoe waterproofer spray, select shoe brands.

MICHAELS
www.michaels.com
Provides all supplies necessary for shoe embroidery: needles, scissors, thread, Fabri-Solvy paper, finger protectors.

Sneakers

CONVERSE
www.converse.com
Manufacturer of the shoes I recommend most for shoe embroidery projects: Converse All Stars, Chuck 70s, Converse Lift Platforms

VANS
www.vans.com
Manufacturer of low-top sneakers that are perfect for some embroidery projects: Vans Authentics

Boots

THURSDAY BOOT COMPANY
https://thursdayboots.com
Manufacturer of high-quality leather boots: Knockout and Legend boots